Pride and Prejudice

Jane Austen

Guide written by John Mahoney

A *Letts* Literature Guide for GCSE

Contents

Plot summary

1 Mr and Mrs Bennet live at Longbourn, Hertfordshire, and have five daughters. Unfortunately, Mr Bennet's estate will not be inherited by his daughters because it is entailed to his cousin, William Collins — a condition of the laws of inheritance.

3 Charles Bingley, a wealthy bachelor, rents Netherfield, which is an estate near Longbourn. With him are his two sisters and his friend, Fitzwilliam Darcy, Lady de Bourgh's nephew.

2 Mrs Bennet is desperate to see her daughters well married to safeguard their future. Mr Collins, a clergyman, has found a living near Rosings, the estate of Lady Catherine de Bourgh.

10 Elizabeth realises that she has misjudged Darcy and that she does love him. However, she now learns that Lydia, her younger sister, has eloped with Wickham. Darcy intervenes to ensure a marriage takes place and that there is no scandal.

11 Bingley and Jane are reunited, and Darcy and Elizabeth marry. His pride has been humbled, and her prejudice erased.

4 At a ball, Mr Darcy offends Elizabeth Bennet with his derogatory remarks about her and her family, while Mr Bingley falls in love with Jane, the eldest of the Bennet sisters.

5 Having already had her pride hurt, Elizabeth is willing to believe the lies that a young man, Wickham, tells her about Darcy. In addition, Darcy and the Bingley sisters persuade Mr Bingley to move from the neighbourhood before he has a chance to propose to Jane.

6 The inane Mr Collins proposes to Elizabeth, but she refuses him. Instead, he marries Elizabeth's friend, Charlotte Lucas.

7 Elizabeth and Darcy meet several times at Rosings, she visiting Charlotte and he his aunt. Darcy falls in love with and proposes to Elizabeth, but in such a proud way that she rejects him and uses the lies spread by Wickham as partial justification for the rejection.

9 Elizabeth, in the company of her aunt and uncle, visits Darcy's house (Pemberley), and meets him by chance. His manner towards her is courteous and warm.

8 Darcy writes to Elizabeth, defending himself and giving the true background to Wickham's accusations.

Who's who in *Pride and Prejudice*

Elizabeth Bennet

Elizabeth, the second of the Bennet daughters and her father's favourite, is the heroine of the novel. She is intelligent, lively, witty and quite capable of holding her own in conversation with someone as well educated as Darcy. She is a strong character with sufficient belief in herself to stand up to such figures as Mr Collins, Lady Catherine de Bourgh and Darcy.

She is deeply affectionate, as witnessed by the sorrow she feels for Jane, whose compassionate nature she much admires. She is perceptive, which helps her to assess accurately the characters of Bingley, his sister and Lady Catherine, but is wrong when she judges Wickham and Darcy. Completely taken in by appearances, she unquestioningly accepts all that Wickham says. She is proud, however, and it is her hurt pride that first makes her prejudiced against Darcy. It is her pride, too, that is flattered by Wickham, who singles her out for personal attention. It is this mixture of pride and prejudice that blunts her judgement of the two men.

Elizabeth reveals a maturity and wisdom beyond that of her parents. She censures her father for not acting responsibly towards his children. She finds irksome her mother's preoccupation with trivia. The atmosphere at home is too confining for her spirits. Above all else, it is Elizabeth's teasing, impulsive disposition which makes her so appealing: Darcy says, near the end of the novel, that it was the 'liveliness' of her mind that first attracted him.

Austen's narrator often shows the situations taking place from Elizabeth's perspective, and it is she that interests the reader more than any other character. Elizabeth and Darcy are the only characters who really develop over the course of the novel.

Jane Bennet

Jane is the eldest and the most beautiful of the Bennet girls. She is so sweet-natured that <u>her</u> <u>desire</u> to <u>find</u> <u>good</u> <u>in</u> <u>everyone</u> <u>is</u> <u>almost</u> <u>a</u> <u>fault</u>. This occasionally leads her to be undiscerning in her assessment of character, and almost prevents her marriage to Bingley. She tries to see virtue in both Wickham and Darcy at the same time. She is <u>an</u> <u>excellent</u> <u>foil</u> <u>for</u> <u>Elizabeth</u>, causing the latter to rethink and justify her often hasty conclusions about people. Their affectionate relationship is one of the most pleasing aspects of the book. Jane <u>keeps</u> <u>her</u> <u>own</u> <u>feelings</u> <u>hidden</u>, and while this helps her to cope when Bingley suddenly leaves the area, it does also lead Darcy into believing that she does not care much for Bingley.

Mr Darcy

Mr Darcy's character is <u>difficult</u> <u>to</u> <u>assess</u> <u>because</u> <u>he</u> <u>is</u> <u>seen</u> <u>almost</u> <u>entirely</u> <u>through</u> <u>Elizabeth's</u> <u>eyes</u>. Therefore it is necessary to look beyond her prejudice to find the true man. Certainly <u>he</u> <u>is</u> <u>proud</u> <u>and</u> <u>unnecessarily</u> <u>rude</u> <u>about</u> <u>Elizabeth</u> <u>when</u> <u>they</u> <u>first</u> <u>meet</u>, but it gradually becomes apparent to the reader that his first impressions of her were wrong and that he becomes increasingly attracted to her. He attributes his haughtiness and social unease to shyness: '<u>We</u> <u>neither</u> <u>of</u> <u>us</u> <u>perform</u> <u>well</u> <u>to</u> <u>strangers</u>', he says to Elizabeth. Shy or not, he is certainly <u>intolerant</u> <u>of</u> <u>other</u> <u>people</u>. Unlike Bingley, who is his opposite in character, Darcy finds Mrs Bennet's behaviour vulgar and embarrassing. He considers Elizabeth's inferior background an impediment to their relationship, even when he first proposes to her.

Darcy's good qualities remain hidden until Elizabeth goes to Pemberley. There she learns from the housekeeper what <u>a</u> <u>fine</u>

master, landlord and brother he is. The full extent of Darcy's good nature is seen in his generosity and sense of responsibility towards Lydia and Wickham. Although a humbler person at the end of the novel, he remains serious. Elizabeth knows that he still is not ready to be teased.

Darcy is the only character other than Elizabeth who evolves during the novel. He becomes less proud and realises that his attitude towards Elizabeth during his first proposal was arrogant and belittling. He is a gentleman, but his conduct on that occasion was not gentlemanly. The success of Elizabeth and Darcy's relationship is based on their growth in self-knowledge and knowledge of each other.

Mr Bingley

Charles Bingley is sociable, uncomplicated and agreeable (as well as being rich, handsome, eligible and young). Unlike his sisters and his friend Darcy, he is not offended by the Bennet family's lack of breeding. He is very attracted to Jane but, being of a compliant disposition, he is easily persuaded by his sisters and his friend Darcy to leave the neighbourhood and return to London. It is only when the relationship between Darcy and Elizabeth is resolved that he and Jane are finally brought together. Bingley and Jane are extremely alike, and it is ironic that the similarities in their natures almost keep them apart.

Mr and Mrs Bennet

Mr Bennet is an intelligent, witty man who nevertheless fails in his duty as a father. Disillusioned by an unhappy marriage, he retreats from his family, in a physical sense by taking refuge in his library and in a moral sense by refusing to take his responsibility as a parent seriously. Instead of guiding and teaching his daughters, he teases and mocks them. Although he is shocked and chastened by

Lydia's elopement, his character does not really change. He reverts to his lazy and selfish life once the crisis is over.

Mrs Bennet is a woman of little understanding or intelligence. She is insensitive to the feelings of others, superficial in thought, and loud in speech. She embarrasses her husband and Elizabeth. Her main occupation is arranging for her five daughters to be married to wealthy husbands. Ironically, her lack of breeding and thoughtlessness almost prevent Jane and Elizabeth from making the satisfactory matches she so much desires for them. Her opinion of Darcy changes immediately on hearing that he is to marry Elizabeth. She is childish in her judgement of people, blaming Mr Collins for the entailment on the Bennet property, and Bingley for Jane's unhappiness.

Lydia Bennet

Lydia is the youngest Bennet daughter and the first to be married, as she proudly announces. Very much like her mother she is self-centred, frivolous and superficial, interested only in clothes, dances and the neighbouring officers. She is shameless about her behaviour with Wickham and quite unaware of the anxiety and trouble she has caused her family.

George Wickham

George Wickham's good looks deceive Elizabeth, her family and the neighbourhood into thinking he is a worthy character. His story about Darcy is sufficient to draw everyone's sympathy and it is accepted uncritically. Elizabeth even excuses him when, for purely mercenary reasons, he transfers his attentions from her to Miss King. His true character is revealed by Darcy only under pressure. Wickham is a spendthrift, a liar and a womaniser. He is persuaded to marry

Lydia (and so prevent a dreadful scandal) only by being given a great sum of money.

Mr Collins

Mr Collins is pompous, insensitive and foolish, and is the object of great satire in the novel. Obsequious to Lady Catherine, he is not perceptive enough to see that she is overbearingly patronising. His lack of self-knowledge and his uncritical mind mean that he does not understand why Elizabeth rejects him, and his feelings are shown to be shallow when he proposes to Charlotte Lucas almost immediately afterwards. His materialistic outlook on life ill befits a clergyman, and his lack of Christian spirit is revealed in the letter he writes to the Bennets after Lydia's marriage.

Caroline Bingley

Miss Bingley is rich, proud and very aware of her social position. Although superficially civil, she scorns the Bennet family for their lack of sophistication and because they have relations in 'trade'. Ironically, we learn that trade is the source of her own inherited wealth. Although one may feel sorry that she is unable to attract the man she wants, she nonetheless remains a hypocrite and a snob.

Lady Catherine de Bourgh

Lady Catherine has an overdeveloped sense of her own importance. She feels that her rank as a lady gives her the right to offer opinions to anyone and everyone on any subject at all. She is not in the habit of being contradicted, surrounded as she is by flatterers like Mr Collins. Her habit of speaking her mind is often an excuse for incivility, and she is so used to having her own way that she is completely taken by surprise when Elizabeth refuses to promise her not to marry Darcy.

Charlotte Lucas

Charlotte, Elizabeth's friend, is a realist. Aware of her poor financial status, she is prepared to marry solely for economic reasons. Although this shocks Elizabeth, there were very few alternatives for a woman in her position. Having made the decision to become Mrs Collins, she carries out her duties correctly and amiably and seems happy. She is sensible to realise that she must keep on good terms with Lady Catherine, and pays the necessary courtesy visits, avoiding confrontation. She cleverly reorganises the rooms at Hunsford to ensure that she sees little of Mr Collins during the day!

Family and friends

Pride and Prejudice is set in a solidly realistic world, with plenty of real places as well as fictional villages and estates. The main characters are therefore placed against a solid background of family, friends and acquaintances. In this way, a leading character is often shadowed by another less important figure who reinforces his/her qualities or failings. Miss Bingley operates at first in tandem with her sister, Mrs Hurst. Colonel Fitzwilliam's behaviour implies that his cousin may have a less forbidding side. The officers, as a group, have qualities of irresponsibility that serve as a background to Wickham's far worse conduct.

In particular, the Bennet family should be examined as a unit, as well as individually. The five sisters break down into three groups: the intelligent and attractive older two, the mousily philosophical and 'artistic' Mary, and the two youngest in wild pursuit of pleasure. All can be seen in different ways as reflections of their parents,

In contrast (and sparing Austen the accusation of snobbery about the middle-classes 'in trade'), are the characters of the excellent Gardiners, thoroughly sensible and kindly, unpretentious and intelligent, even though Mr Gardiner is an attorney's son 'in a respectable line of trade'.

About the author

Jane Austen

Jane Austen was born on 16 December 1775 at the Rectory in Steventon, a small town in Hampshire. Her parents were the Reverend George Austen and his wife Cassandra. She was the seventh child born to the couple, who went on to have a total of eight children. She had six brothers and one sister, Cassandra, to whom she remained close throughout her life. Austen lived in Steventon until she was 25, and subsequently moved to Bath, Southampton and then back to Chawton in Hampshire, where she died on 18 July 1817.

Austen had barely five years of formal education, which comprised of being tutored for a year by a Mrs Cawley in Oxford, then in Southampton. After they both fell ill (and Jane nearly died), she and her elder sister, Cassandra, attended the Abbey School in Reading. Austen was part of a family that loved to act, and the Rectory barn was transformed into a theatre in which Austen and her relatives would produce plays to entertain themselves, friends and neighbours. Austen's social circle included members of the clergy and landed gentry. It was from her father, her brothers and their relatives that Austen gained most of her education, and from reading not only to herself but aloud to the family in the evenings as a form of entertainment.

After writing three notebooks of burlesques of contemporary novels, which were clearly intended to be family entertainment, Austen began writing her first novel. It was written as a series of letters and was entitled *Elinor and Marianne*. A year later, in 1797, it was retitled *Sense and Sensibilty*. Austen also worked on another piece of literature between 1796 and 1797, with the working title of *First Impressions*. She later revised the manuscript and renamed it *Pride and Prejudice*, a title believed to be taken from the novel *Cecilia,* by one of Austen's favourite authors, Fanny Burney: 'The whole unfortunate business [was] the result of Pride and Prejudice'. Austen then worked on a novel she called *Susan*, but which was published under the title *Northanger Abbey*. This was intended to be a satire of the Gothic novels of the time, such as the extremely popular *Castle of Otranto* (1764) by Horace Walpole.

In 1801, when her father retired, Austen moved to Bath with her family. However, when her father died in 1805, Austen stayed with friends and family in Bath, London, Clifton and Warwickshire before spending four years living in Southampton with her mother and sister. Little is known about her private life, but it is believed that she accepted a marriage proposal from one Harris Bigg-Wither only to change her mind the next day. She never married. In 1809, her brother Edward provided Austen, her mother and sister with a cottage in Chawton, Hampshire, where she lived until her death.

It was while living in Chawton that Austen revised her three earlier novels and wrote her other three: *Mansfield Park*, *Emma* and *Persuasion*. None of Austen's novels were published at the time they were written, and even when they were published several were initially done so anonymously. *Sense and Sensibility* was published in 1811, followed by *Pride and Prejudice* in 1813. *Mansfield Park* was published in 1814 and *Emma* in 1815. *Northanger Abbey* and *Persuasion* were published posthumously by her brother Henry. Her final novel, *Sandtion*, remains unpublished.

In 1816, Austen became unwell. At the time it was impossible to diagnose what was wrong, but the symptoms suggest that her condition may have been Addison's disease. She was put under the care of an expert surgeon in 1817, but nothing could be done. She died on 18 July 1817 and was buried in Winchester Cathedral. She is remembered most for her comedies of manners and her satirical narrative style.

Although Jane Austen does not explicitly mention the social and political background in her writing, the late eighteenth and early nineteenth century was a time of great social change and revolution. *Pride and Prejudice* was originally written in 1797 and was set in late eighteenth century England. It is important for the reader to look at why none of the major world events of the time are clearly referred to. Is it because Jane Austen simply chose to write social satires about microcosms of society or was she actually blissfully unaware of what transpired outside of her small social circle?

The American War of Independence had ended in 1784 and the French Revolution had begun in 1789. Both events brought about great social and political change, and yet there is no mention of them in Austen's work. In 1792 France declared itself a republic, and in 1793 declared war on Britain. The French monarch, Louis XVI, and his wife Marie Antoinette were guillotined. With the monarchy overthrown, France fell into social anarchy as a new order was established and the people of France became *citizens*. This was an unspeakably awful time for the aristocracy in France, with many of them being beheaded for crimes against the new republic. Britain feared similar reprisals towards the ruling elite. Between 1800 and 1815 the Napoleonic Wars were waged, and continued the revolutionary feeling, until they ended with Napoleon's defeat by Nelson at the Battle of Waterloo in 1815. During this time, the French army had undertaken a series of aggressive campaigns in Europe.

The novel does include some inferences to life outside Austen's England, but these are generally used to put events and characters into social context. In the 1790s, the British army was moving around the country in preparation for the very real threat of invasion. The army arriving in *Pride and Prejudice* is like an invasion of the small community of the novel, and causes much excitement among the ladies. Are the men a welcome injection of masculinity in the exceedingly feminine world the novel inhabits? For example, the arrival of the military officers in Meryton is a key moment – it heralds the arrival of George Wickham, a key player in the novel. Consider whether Wickham is more objectionable to the reader because he simply uses the army as a means to his own ends (as he does with everyone and everything), when he should be defending the country.

Austen only refers explicity to the events of the outside world once during the novel. This is in the last chapter where she mentions how Lydia and Wickham were always looking for a cheap situation 'even when the restoration of the peace dismissed them to a home'. The 'peace' she refers to was a brief interval during the European War. Other than this, the social situation can only be determined through different characters' behaviour. Darcy and Lady Catherine de Bourgh are of the landed gentry, and therefore tradition and background are of immense importance to them. Miss Bingley has great concerns about other people's social backgrounds and 'worth', and yet the reader discovers that her father made his money in industry in the North of England. There is a sense of fear in the social elite in the novel about 'lesser mortals' invading their social circle and ultimately their bloodline.

Look carefully at the way in which Austen portrays the English aristocracy. Surely the events in the outside world emphasise the mindless preoccupations of some of the more ridiculous characters in the novel? Is it possible that these characters cannot see outside their own little world?

An aristocratic house from Austen's time.

Love and marriage

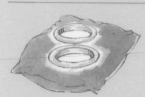

Although *Pride and Prejudice* is chiefly concerned with marriage, there are very few uses of the word love. When the term does appear, Austen's omniscient narrator and the more sensible characters generally express scepticism. The phrase 'violently in love' is described by Mrs Gardiner as 'hackneyed, doubtful and indefinite' (Chapter 25), used to refer to anything from a short acquaintance to a 'strong attachment'. Overall, Austen seems uncertain of the lasting qualities of passionate love, and convinced that it is not a strong enough basis for marriage. In *Pride and Prejudice*, true love is rational as well as emotional. It is based on mutual esteem, respect and gratitude, and arises from a clear-sighted understanding of the other person's character. Passion is part of true love, but must be controlled. True love has the power to change people: Elizabeth attributes Darcy's loss of pride to 'love, ardent love'. It also has the power to persuade people: conscious of Darcy's regard for her, Elizabeth grows to love him partly through gratitude for his love.

Austen is interested in the way people select their partners. *Pride and Prejudice* includes four weddings, so there is plenty of scope to explore this theme. Indeed, three clearly different kinds of marriage are described. There is the mercenary marriage brought about entirely for economic reasons. The union between Charlotte and Mr Collins is a good example of this. Charlotte is already pessimistic about finding happiness in marriage, and believes she may as well marry to guarantee her financial security. For a woman without personal fortune, this was an attractive basis for marriage.

Almost completely in contrast to this prudent view is the marriage based solely on passion and physical attraction. Lydia and Wickham make such a marriage, as did Mr and Mrs Bennet years before. The success of such a union can be judged by looking at the relationship between Mr and Mrs Bennet. Once the excitement of 'youth and beauty' has faded, these two people find that they do not understand or even like each other. Given the character of Wickham, it should not seem strange that he held out for as good an economic settlement as possible before agreeing to marry Lydia, but the initial attraction between the two had everything to do with passion and physical attraction and little to do with mutual understanding of character.

Somewhere in between these two views of marriage lies the ideal. This is characterised by the relationships between Darcy and Elizabeth, and between Jane and Bingley. While the characters in these two pairings are very different, both relationships are 'rationally founded', based on 'excellent understanding' and 'general similarity of feeling and taste' (Chapter 55). Austen believes that in relationships, reason should dominate emotion. Both partners must have compatibility of interests, temperament and intelligence for a marriage to work well.

Money and financial security

Austen lived in a mercenary world, and this is reflected in the novel. No secret is made of the need to marry for money. A woman who has no fortune must look for a man who has, and vice versa — something which even Elizabeth admits.

Elizabeth's own situation as a single woman is precarious: her father's estate is entailed through the male line, and therefore she needs to marry well so as to secure a stable future for herself, her unmarried sisters and her mother after her father's death. She criticises Charlotte, not for marrying a wealthy man, but for marrying solely for money. On the other hand, she quite accepts Wickham's motives for transferring his attentions from herself to Miss King, a rich woman. Mrs Bennet's fixation with marriage can be largely explained by the poor financial position of her daughters.

Money plays a crucial role in ensuring the final happy endings. Were it not for Darcy's generosity in settling a large sum of money on Wickham (thereby averting the scandal that would have erupted if no marriage had taken place), none of the Bennet girls would have stood much chance of marrying. You should note that Elizabeth's reward for being our heroine is more money than all of her sisters.

Pride and prejudice

It is frequently difficult to separate cause and effect with regard to this major theme. Darcy's pride in his family, social class and connections leads him to be prejudiced against people of Elizabeth's (comparatively lesser) social standing. His arrogant treatment of Elizabeth offends her innate pride and, in turn, prejudices her against him.

The novel examines the nature of pride. Darcy is censured for his pride by public opinion in general and by Elizabeth in particular. This disapproval is deserved, as his uncivil behaviour at the Netherfield ball offends the etiquette of the time (although Charlotte Lucas thinks his social rank gives him the right to haughty manners). Darcy himself attributes his lack of ease to shyness, not pride, but he does admit to the fault of snobbery: he is prejudiced against Elizabeth's social inferiority.

Elizabeth, too, is guilty of pride. Apart from feeling an immediate dislike towards Darcy because of his supercilious attitude, her prejudice against him initially arises from hurt pride: he makes insensitive remarks about her appearance. Prejudiced against Darcy, she is easily deceived into believing badly of him by Wickham. It is interesting to compare how she views Darcy before and after she discovers the truth of his character. Before receiving the letter which changes everything, she can see no further than his pride: 'his abominable pride'. At Pemberley, after the revelations of his letter, she is 'amazed at the alteration in his manner', an alteration due partly to less pride on his part but also to less prejudice on hers.

Class and etiquette

Austen was writing in the late eighteenth and early nineteenth century (*Pride and Prejudice* was first published in 1813), largely about the landed gentry of England — people whose wealth was inherited, rather than worked for. This class covered a wide range in terms of wealth and property (from the near-aristocracy to quite humble landowners), but all shared certain social attitudes. It was common to look down on those in trade, though *Pride and Prejudice* contains many examples of people only recently gentrified, and of social intercourse between the classes.

Austen describes the attitudes, social behaviour and preoccupations of the gentry in detail. They are often snobbish and mercenary, as well as censorious of those who contravene their social and moral standards. Strict etiquette governs such matters as introducing oneself as, or to, a new neighbour. The way people behave can qualify or disqualify them as members of the social group. The word Austen most frequently uses in this context is 'civility'.

Darcy's feelings about Elizabeth's inferior social situation are compounded by her parents' and her younger sisters' behaviour in public. Her mother is loud, brash and tactless and her father embarrassing and openly mocking of his family. Her sister Lydia, at fifteen, is superficial, flirtatious and her behaviour unrefined. Her sister Mary is pious and boring. Only Jane has any notion of how to behave appropriately in society.

The role of women

The role of women in Austen's time was quite unlike that of today. Women were invariably subservient to men and were expected to become 'accomplished' in such pursuits as art, reading and music. These were deemed to make a woman more attractive and finer company. To an extent Austen mocks this, as her central female character Elizabeth Bennet is admired more for her ready wit and intelligence than how well she plays the piano or sings. The Bingley women are shown to be accomplished, but are unpleasant snobs who ridicule others. They have been given all the opportunities that life offers but have failed to become decent human beings. The Bennets have had to rely on their father to educate them (as Austen did herself) and at times he has failed them. Considering that he is aware that the girls need to be attractive marriage prospects due to the entailment, it reflects badly on him that they have not had a governess.

It is both highly relevant and to an extent amusing that the novel follows the prospects of a group of sisters. The novel's chief concern is the fate of women in the 'marriage market' and the qualities that recommend them to possible partners. Only the two eldest Bennet girls are sensible and attractive, the others being either frivolous and silly or, in Mary's case, less attractive and therefore determined to show superior intelligence. What does this say about the society they live in? Women were excluded from a large number of activities and were expected to keep house and keep quiet. They could not visit a new member of the town until the male figure in the house had called upon them first. Hence Mrs Bennet's distress that her husband intially refuses to call upon Mr Bingley.

One of the main preoccupations of a woman's life would be making a suitable marriage. Generally, Austen novels revolve around this idea and what constitutes a 'good' marriage. In the late eighteenth century women were to an extent viewed as commodities, and marriage would be as much a 'business transaction' as a 'love-match'. Women were judged on their wealth and position in society. Austen believed that marriage without love was a terrible notion, but fully acknowledged the need for an equal match in terms of wealth/social status, love and being compatible in terms of character.

Although beauty would have been prized, a father being able to present a prospective husband with a generous dowry was equally important. Problems arose when, as in *Pride and Prejudice*, the female line would not inherit upon the father's death. This increased the pressure of making a 'good match', as failure to do so could result in their becoming homeless and having to rely on the charity of others. The only alternative to marriage in Austen's time for a respectable girl would be to become a governess but this would mean a life of drudgery.

Four marriages take place during the course of the novel and the narrator is deeply sardonic towards those for whom love is not even a consideration. It seems somehow ironic that Lydia, marrying for passion, is chastised so strongly and could destroy the prospects of the other sisters. In many eighteenth century novels her elopement would be exciting and thrilling, but here it is reviled as destructive and supremely selfish. Austen shows the importance of chastity, family background, social status and wealth in the single woman in eighteenth century England.

Text commentary

Pride and Prejudice was originally published in three volumes, although most modern editions number the chapters straight through from 1 to 61. Chapter numbers are given here, but the Quick Quizzes are placed at the end of Austen's original volumes to remind you of this earlier structure.

Chapter 1

> **❝***It is a truth universally acknowledged, that a single man in possession of a good fortune, must be in want of a wife***❞**

In the opening sentence Austen sums up the theme of her book. <u>The narrator is being heavily ironic</u>, implying that very often parents with daughters assume that single men of 'good fortune' want to get married, when in fact it may be the last thing they want.

Explore

Look at the opening of the BBC film version, and the importance placed on Mr Bingley looking at and deciding to purchase Netherfield.

In this first chapter we are introduced to Mr and Mrs Bennet and quickly, through dialogue, we have a good idea of their characters and their marriage. Look at the way <u>**Mr Bennet teases his wife**</u>: he knows that Mr Bingley's arrival is of great importance to his daughters' marital expectations, yet he pretends to be disinterested and mocks her seriousness. <u>**For Mrs Bennet the matter of making social contact with all eligible bachelors is a very serious one**</u>. The reader is shown this exchange from an ironic standpoint, through the eyes of Mr Bennet and the omniscient narrator.

The characters of Mr and Mrs Bennet are summed up in the last paragraph of the chapter. Their marriage cannot have been close if 23 years have been <u>'insufficient to make his wife understand his character'</u>.

Notice the **strict code of behaviour** of this time period. It would have seemed discourteous for women to visit a new neighbour without previous formal introduction by the head of the household. Mr Bennet has to visit Bingley and introduce himself before any social contact between the two families can take place.

Chapter 2

> **Mr Bennet was among the earliest of those who waited on Mr Bingley.**

Mr Bennet is very sarcastic about his daughters Kitty and Mary, and again mocks his wife. It seems that **he enjoys teasing his wife, and has a low opinion of some of his own daughters**. The fact that he has to derive pleasure from his family in this way suggests that he is not very happily married and that, really, he is disaffected with his family life.

Explore

Note how Austen is showing the reader the consequences of making a marriage that is not based on respect and understanding.

Mrs Bennet is irritable when she thinks that her plans are going to be frustrated by her husband's refusal to pay a call on Bingley. Moments later, she has a complete change of mood on hearing the good news that he has already visited Netherfield. This is a good example of **her 'uncertain temper'**, described by Austen at the end of the previous chapter. The humour in this chapter is derived from Mr Bennet deliberately withholding information from the over-anxious Mrs Bennet and pretending to misunderstand her comments.

The most serious of the Bennet girls, Mary attempts to derive wisdom from reading books. Unlike her father and her sister Elizabeth, she lacks the perception to judge people by their behaviour, so her pronouncements, when she makes them, sound empty and irrelevant. Look at Chapters 5 and 47 for examples of this.

Chapter 3

> *To be fond of dancing was a certain step towards falling in love*

Explore

How, in Chapter 18, do Elizabeth and Darcy make use of this social convention?

Austen is ironic here about the assumptions made by general society. Yet there is truth in the narrator's statement: in the late eighteenth and early nineteenth centuries, a dance was the only way that two people could have a private conversation in public. In this way, Austen emphasises the fact that **the individual is a part of society**, answerable to others as much as to him or herself.

The aim of Mrs Bennet's life is summarised at the beginning of Chapter 3: **'If I can but see one of my daughters happily settled'**. In this respect she seems to be more aware of her duties as a parent than her husband. Where she falls down is in her failure to appreciate the dangers of finding an unsuitable partner — something her own marriage should have taught her. **For Mrs Bennet, a 'suitable' husband is a wealthy one**.

> *His character was decided.*

Austen satirises public opinion here. The rumour of Mr Darcy's wealth is taken as fact, and general opinion is instantly formed that he has 'handsome features' and a 'noble mein'. Neverthless, that opinion is quickly altered on the strength of his unsociable behaviour. Heightened by contrast with Bingley's amiable behaviour, **Darcy's arrogance is condemned, prejudice against him sets in**, and his appearance is rapidly seen to alter to a 'forbidding, disagreeable countenance'.

Darcy's and Bingley's characters are contrasted and Meryton society saterised. It seems that a person's affability is determined by their willingness to dance.

Explore

This is Elizabeth's and Darcy's first meeting and the beginning of all the confusions that arise. Can you tell why the novel was originally called *First Impressions*?

The dialogue in this chapter quite forcefully reveals **Darcy's pride**. Later he maintains it was shyness that led to his awkward behaviour at the ball. However, it is hard to justify his comments on such grounds, especially the remarks he makes about Elizabeth: **'She is tolerable; but not handsome enough to tempt me'**. Later, when he first proposes to her, his attitude is just as proud, but at that point he explains his reasons for such offensive behaviour: 'His sense of her inferiority ... of the family obstacles ... were dwelt on'.

The society Austen describes was very quick to judge on appearances. Just as Darcy had been judged by the assembly, so **Elizabeth quickly makes up her mind**. Her reaction to his insult, making a joke of it to her family and friends, shows that she is resilient and lively.

Chapter 4

❝He is just what a young man ought to be❞

Jane and Elizabeth are contrasted in this chapter. **Jane is shown to accept people at face value**. She is impressed with Bingley because of his good breeding and manners. Elizabeth mocks her a little when she says: 'His character is thereby complete'. **Elizabeth**, more lively and more cynical about people and their intentions, **feels that judgement should be more discerning**. Yet it is she, not Jane, who is later guilty of being deceived by appearances — note her ready acceptance of Wickham later in the novel.

Elizabeth draws attention to Jane's kind nature, but **Jane's ability to see good in everyone affects her judgement**. She and Bingley are very alike; they are shown to be generous and unassuming, a perfect match. However, their mutual unwillingness to think ill of people almost prevents their marriage. Jane's view that Miss Bingley is 'charming' is not shared by Elizabeth. As we get to know Miss Bingley better, it is obvious that <u>Elizabeth's 'quickness of observation'</u> has given her a truer assessment of Miss Bingley's character — again, that faculty will be less obvious when it comes to judging Wickham.

Manners and breeding were of considerable importance in upper-class circles. They play a major role in the novel, as <u>the Bennet family's lack of breeding</u> is a major impediment to the progress of Elizabeth's and Darcy's relationship. To belong to a family whose fortune was made in trade was to belong to an inferior class. It is ironic to see Miss Bingley's disdain for the Bennet family because they have relations in <u>'trade'</u>. In Austen's society, Miss Bingley and her sister would have been called <u>'ladies'</u> as they fulfil all the requirements: they have money, beauty and are accomplished. However, although Elizabeth notes with irony that they are 'in every respect entitled to think well of themselves', their subsequent behaviour, particularly with regard to the Bennets, is far from 'ladylike'. <u>'Manners' are a better indication of 'breeding' than is birth</u>.

Explore

Contrast the snobbish and proud Lady Catherine de Bourgh with the friendly, helpful Gardiners. Look at Darcy's attitude towards them.

Darcy and Bingley are also compared in this chapter. The two men are described as being quite opposite in temperament: <u>Bingley is easy-going and sociable; Darcy is complicated and distant</u>. Of the two, Darcy is the more intelligent and Bingley respects his

judgement. To illustrate this contrast, their impressions of the ball are very different: 'Bingley had never met with pleasanter people or prettier girls in his life; every body had been most kind and attentive to him … Darcy, on the contrary, had seen a collection of people in whom there was little beauty and no fashion, for none of whom he felt the smallest interest'.

Chapter 5

> **The distinction had perhaps been felt too strongly.**

Austen uses satire to describe Sir William Lucas's new position as a gentleman. In a society clearly divided by rank, he regards it as important to sever all connection with his past life as a businessman. Although Elizabeth mocks him gently, he is not an unpleasant character.

It is left to Jane to find something good to say about Darcy. She is the only one to suggest that his reserve is due more to shyness than pride. This is the reason he gives for his behaviour later in the novel and, when we meet his sister, she too is very shy in company. Mrs Bennet automatically jumps to the conclusion that Darcy is rude and haughty. Charlotte Lucas's suggestion that Darcy's rank justifies his pride tells us a little about her attitude to men of fortune. This in turn prepares us for her response when Mr Collins proposes.

Chapter 6

> **The ladies of Longbourn soon waited on those of Netherfield.**

Charlotte's remark that Jane 'may lose the opportunity of fixing' Bingley because of her 'composure of temper and uniform cheerfulness', is proved correct later in the novel. This is an excellent example of the care Austen takes to construct a plot in which every comment is significant and where every character plays an intrinsic role. Charlotte is more worldly than Jane, and is aware of the importance of appearance in a society which lays so much stress on behaviour.

Explore

Look at Chapter 35 to see that this is exactly the reason Darcy gives for believing that Jane had no special affection for Bingley.

> **❝**Happiness in marriage is entirely a matter of chance.**❞**

Charlotte's views on marriage are very different from Elizabeth's. In marrying, <u>Charlotte</u> <u>is</u> <u>chiefly</u> <u>concerned</u> <u>with</u> <u>obtaining</u> <u>a</u> <u>good</u> <u>financial</u> <u>match:</u> <u>sentiment</u> <u>plays</u> <u>little</u> <u>part</u>. She makes it clear that she sees marriage in terms of economics. Her expectations are no higher than that. Again, note the way that Austen prepares us for future events. Knowing her views, we should not be surprised when Charlotte accepts Mr Collins's proposal.

Elizabeth does not think that Charlotte, with her cynical view of marriage, is being serious. Notice the dramatic irony in her comment: 'you would never act in this way yourself'. Again, Elizabeth's judgement will prove unsound. Elizabeth feels that <u>marriage</u> <u>should</u> <u>be</u> <u>a</u> <u>union</u> <u>based</u> <u>on</u> <u>mutual</u> <u>knowledge</u> <u>and</u> <u>understanding</u>. She protests that Jane does not yet know Bingley well enough to have decided whether she is in love with him or not.

Meanwhile Darcy, while maintaining that <u>Elizabeth's</u> <u>manners</u> <u>are</u> <u>'not</u> <u>those</u> <u>of</u> <u>the</u> <u>fashionable</u> <u>world'</u>, is nevertheless attracted by her <u>'playfulness'</u>. Unbeknown to her, his interest is increasing. She is lively and teasing towards him, determined to use the weapon of her wit to face his 'satirical eye'. But Elizabeth, too, has her pride, and <u>she</u> <u>will</u> <u>not</u> <u>let</u> <u>it</u> <u>be</u> <u>thought</u> <u>that</u> <u>she</u> <u>is</u> <u>hunting</u> <u>for</u> <u>a</u> <u>partner</u>. However, by refusing to dance with Darcy, she only increases her attractiveness. He sees spirit and pride in her character, and an independence of mind which appeals to him.

Miss Bingley expresses contempt at the dullness of the society before her. However, her contempt is also occasioned by jealousy. Darcy has changed his opinion of Elizabeth: before, he thought her merely 'tolerable'; now,

he thinks <u>she has 'a pair of fine eyes' and is 'pretty'</u>.
The narrator speaks through Darcy's consciousness, therefore
the reader knows that his opinion of Elizabeth is changing.
Elizabeth, however, remains completely unaware of his change
of feelings. Caroline Bingley is surprised when Darcy contradicts
her opinions.

Chapter 7

> **"** *I remember the time when I liked a red coat myself.* **"**

Catherine (Kitty) and Lydia seem very impressed with
superficial appearances, such as the 'regimentals of an
ensign', proving the earlier observation that <u>'their minds
were more vacant than their sisters''</u>. It becomes
apparent that Lydia is just like her mother: silly and vain.
As you read the sections where Lydia and Kitty are
mercilessly satirised, consider what the reader is supposed to
think of Mr Bennet, who thinks his own daughters are 'two of
the silliest girls in the country'.

Mr Bennet is again ironic in his conversation with his wife.
In almost no respect do they agree and again he has fun at
her expense. Mrs Bennet's lack of perception and decorum is
evident in the way she defends Lydia. Despite her lack of
intelligence, she has the guile to formulate a scheme to keep
Jane at Netherfield overnight.

Elizabeth's <u>independence of spirit</u> is again shown by her
decision to walk to Netherfield in order to visit her sister.
The effect of the walk on her appearance is not lost on
Darcy (he admires <u>'the brilliancy which exercise had
given her complexion'</u>), although the Bingley sisters
are horrified at such <u>unorthodox behaviour</u>.

Chapter 8

> **"** *with such a father and mother, and such low connections, I am afraid there is no chance of it* **"**

The Bingley sisters' concern for Jane is shown to be superficial. They are also critical of Elizabeth's appearance and behaviour when she is out of the room, and are scornful of the Bennets' social rank. Miss Bingley attempts to impress Darcy with compliments and praise, but it is Elizabeth's intelligence and independence of thought which he notices. Jane's health continues to give cause for concern.

Notice <u>the</u> <u>importance</u> of <u>family</u> <u>status</u> <u>and</u> <u>background</u> <u>when</u> <u>choosing</u> <u>a</u> <u>partner</u> <u>for</u> <u>marriage</u>, and how different Bingley and Darcy's views are on the subject. Bingley's kind nature contrasts with his sisters' spitefulness, and he tries to soften the sharpness of Miss Bingley's words with sympathetic remarks of his own.

Bingley's description of **'accomplished'** women gives an insight into the kinds of activities upper-class women undertook at the time. Theirs was a gentle, delicate existence, and Elizabeth's behaviour, walking (through mud) to Netherfield, would not have been considered lady-like. We can sense, though, Austen's humour at the kind of 'accomplishments' the Bingleys describe. <u>Elizabeth's physical and mental energy is, we feel, admired by the author</u>.

Chapter 9

> **"** *That is my idea of good breeding* **"**

<u>Mrs Bennet's lack of breeding</u> is apparent when she quizzes Bingley on his intentions to leave or stay at Netherfield. Then she

reveals her hostility towards Darcy and makes herself look foolish by misunderstanding his comment about country people. Elizabeth, 'blushing for her mother', tries to change the subject. Mrs Bennet is unaware that people consider her ridiculous and unrefined. <u>There is an underlying assumption that country life and country people are dull</u>. As if to confirm Darcy's feelings about the narrowness of country life, Mrs Bennet boasts in a childish, unintelligent way about the number of families in the Bennets' social circle.

Darcy cannot help but be impressed with Elizabeth's wit. She is forced to try and lighten the awkward atmosphere created by her mother's boastful and tactless conversation. In the final sentence of this chapter we learn that Darcy will not join the others in criticising Elizabeth.

Chapter 10

> *But do you always write such charming long letters to her, Mr Darcy?*

The contrast between Darcy and Bingley is again highlighted by the description of their different styles of writing. <u>Letters form an important part of the novel</u>. One of their chief uses is to reveal character. Darcy's measured style of writing reflects his staid, proud character. Bingley's more careless style of writing is in keeping with his agreeable and impulsive nature. Bingley's easy-going nature finds arguments unpleasant. He does not share Darcy and Elizabeth's pleasure in witty repartee. Note that it was quite common in Austen's time to write <u>epistolary novels</u>, novels written in the form of letters.

<u>Elizabeth's prejudice blinds her to Darcy's true feelings</u>. She is unaware that his interest in her is based on growing admiration. She mistakenly believes he disapproves of her. Not that she cares, for she still dislikes

him: **'She liked him too little to care for his approbation'**.
So when he asks her to dance a reel — a country dance —
Elizabeth's interpretation of Mr Darcy's request is that he wishes
to insult her by implying that she, a country bumpkin, would
enjoy such a dance. **Her pride is hurt**. As you read this incident,
remember that Darcy is battling with the knowledge that he is
falling in love with Elizabeth, and that her status prevents him
from believing that there is any future in it.

Chapter 11

❝❝ *I hope I never ridicule what is wise*
or good. **❞❞**

Elizabeth is Austen's mouthpiece here. Consider the characters
Elizabeth/Austen satirises: Mr Collins, Miss Bingley, Lady
Catherine. It is not only their foolishness and 'inconsistencies'
that she mocks, but also their hypocrisy, incivility and lack of
'true' breeding.

Notice how seriously Darcy takes himself. He makes a
conscious effort not to put himself into a situation where he is
open to ridicule or teasing by a 'strong understanding' such
as Elizabeth's. She teases Darcy about his self-
consciousness: **'Mr Darcy has no defect. He owns it
himself without disguise.'** Consider his behaviour
towards Elizabeth when she has rejected his proposal, and his
behaviour towards Wickham after the elopement. Can it really be
said that Darcy knows himself as well as he thinks?

Chapter 12

❝❝ *On Sunday, after morning service, the*
separation, so agreeable to almost all,
took place. **❞❞**

You will notice the absence of dialogue in this short chapter. As an interlude between two stages of the story, it serves as a brief summary. No time is wasted with speech; instead there is a rapid survey of the characters' feelings and attitudes.

Chapter 13

> **❝I have reason to expect an addition to our family party.❞**

Mr Collins's letter reveals him to be <u>pompous, condescending, fawning and insensitive</u>. The Bennet family are divided as to his qualities. Mrs Bennet is favourably impressed and optimistic that he will be advantageous to the girls; Jane thinks his motives worthy. Mr Bennet and Elizabeth see the true man.

Chapter 14

> **❝She had even condescended to advise him to marry as soon as he could❞**

To the amusement of Mr Bennet, Mr Collins describes his luck and gratitude in being the recipient of Lady Catherine's patronage. He bathes in her reflected 'glory'. To Mr Bennet, <u>Mr Collins is an absurd figure,</u> who lays himself open to ridicule through his pomposity and blind deference to Lady Catherine. Significantly, Mrs Bennet accepts Mr Collins at face value and even approves of him. Mr Bennet, aware that Mr Collins is foolish and pompous, has one hope for him: that he will be absurd enough to provide constant amusement. The fact that Lady Catherine tolerates this ridiculous fawning suggests that she is not a particularly sensible person.

Chapter 15

> **"Mr Collins was not a sensible man"**

By way of summarising Mr Collins's character, Austen describes him as: 'a mixture of pride and obsequiousness, self-importance and humility'. His decision to marry one of the Bennet girls is based on the assumption that <u>they are in no position (financially) to refuse him</u>. He obviously does not place love and compatibility high on his list of reasons for marriage. Note Mrs Bennet's reaction to Mr Collins. What is wrong with her sole concern being to find a husband with a fortune for her daughters?

Notice the way that Wickham is first described and contrasted with Mr Collins: 'His appearance was greatly in his favour; he had all the best part of beauty, a fair countenance, a good figure, and very pleasing address.' The repetition of the word 'appearance' is, however, an early-warning signal that <u>Wickham is not necessarily the man he seems to be</u>.

Chapter 16

> **"Elizabeth was the happy woman by whom he finally seated himself"**

The attractiveness of Wickham is increased by the ease of his conversation, which contrasts with the pedestrian nature of Mr Collins's talk. He cunningly prompts Elizabeth's curiosity by the use of the emotive word 'scandalous'. Wickham does not strike her as indiscreet in relating this story to a comparative stranger. <u>It shows how much Elizabeth dislikes Darcy that she is willing to believe Wickham's story</u>. This makes her suspend her usual scepticism and judgement.

Wickham implies that he has not brought the matter out in public because of his own sense of honour. Elizabeth finds Wickham's story plausible because his manner is attractive and open: the opposite of Darcy's. Yet she cannot believe that a gentleman such as Darcy could break his father's promise. Surely his pride would make him behave honestly? However, Wickham suggests that other 'impulses', such as jealousy and hatred, have characterised Darcy's behaviour towards him.

Explore

Why does Elizabeth choose to believe Wickham?

To the list of Darcy's faults, Wickham now adds hypocrisy. When Elizabeth asks how an agreeable man such as Bingley can like such a bad character, Wickham says that Darcy changes his behaviour to suit his company.

Chapter 17

> **❝Elizabeth related to Jane the next day, what had passed between Mr Wickham and herself.❞**

Jane, wanting to think well of Darcy, suggests that perhaps the full story has not yet been told. <u>For once, her desire to see good in everyone is justified</u>.

The invitations to the Netherfield Ball are distributed in this chapter. Balls and dancing were the major social activity of people of this class, especially when in the country. A ball would provide the main topic of conversation for a week beforehand and for days afterwards.

Chapter 18

> **❝She had dressed with more than usual care❞**

A dance, one of the chief ways a couple could talk fairly intimately in private, could be a source of misery with a boring

Explore

Notice the use of picture imagery, 'illustration', 'sketch', and 'likeness', in Elizabeth's assessment of Darcy's character.

partner. Compare Elizabeth's dances with Mr Collins and with Darcy. Although she would never admit to enjoying it, Elizabeth's conversation with Darcy is animated. Darcy is reluctant to give his side of the story. Blinded by prejudice, Elizabeth does not see this as virtuous.

Darcy is alarmed by Sir William Lucas's assumption that Jane and Bingley are to be married. As he later explains, he believes Jane is indifferent to Bingley and is therefore alarmed that his friend might be rushing into a marriage he will later regret. Notice Mrs Bennet's indiscretion in discussing the possibility of marriage between Jane and Bingley. Ironically, this directly causes the disruption in their relationship – Darcy, alarmed by the schemes he overhears, persuades his friend to leave quickly for London.

Charlotte's attitude towards marriage is shown in her remarks to Elizabeth about Darcy. To her, Darcy should not be dismissed in favour of Wickham, because the former is <u>'a man ten times his consequence'</u>.

<u>'It is particularly incumbent on those who never change their opinion, to be secure of judging properly at first.'</u> Elizabeth's statement is unconsciously ironic. It is she who has not judged Darcy 'properly at first' and her prejudice continues to cloud her judgement. She will not believe Miss Bingley because she suspects her motives. So complete is her prejudice against Darcy and in favour of Wickham that she will not even trust Bingley's mild reaction against Wickham's character, as reported to her by Jane.

Mr Collins, with his strange mixture of 'self-importance and humility', is anxious to introduce himself to Darcy because of their mutual connection — Lady Catherine is Darcy's aunt. Elizabeth, fearing that Darcy will regard this as an 'impertinent freedom', tries to dissuade him. Mr Collins believes that his

status as a clergyman places him 'as equal in point of dignity' to Mr Darcy. He is so thick-skinned that he does not notice the scorn with which Darcy treats him. However, **Elizabeth <u>is</u> <u>sensitive</u> <u>to</u> <u>Darcy's</u> <u>contempt</u>** for Mr Collins. Her pride is wounded here, perhaps because, subconsciously, she cares about what Darcy thinks.

Chapter 19

> *Almost as soon as I entered the house I singled you out as the companion of my future life.*

In listing the reasons why he should marry, Mr Collins is insensitive to Elizabeth's feelings, making no mention of love, affection, respect or compatibility. It is a tribute to Elizabeth's strength of character that she manages to remain civil in her reply to him.

Explore

Where is the humour in Mr Collins choosing Elizabeth 'almost as soon' as he arrived?

In this chapter Austen preserves a delicate balance in the reader's reactions. Elizabeth has already been established as the main focus of the reader's sympathy and this is a painful scene for her; on the other hand, the behaviour of Mr Collins is outrageously comic. The reader therefore exists in a state of amused exasperation. Again you should look for the sources of humour in Mr Collins.

Chapter 20

> *An unhappy alternative is before you, Elizabeth.*

This chapter contains one of the most amusing of Mr Bennet's witticisms. Beginning with mock-solemnity (above), he moves on to claim that, whatever choice she makes, she will never again

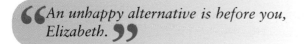

see one of her parents. **'Your mother will never see you again if you do not marry Mr Collins, and I will never see you again if you do.'** Elizabeth smiles; so does the reader, but is it responsible parenting?

Chapter 21

> *The discussion of Mr Collins's offer was now nearly at an end*

Caroline Bingley's letter shows the writer's **unkind and malicious** character, as it is intended to hurt the recipient. It also closes one phase of the novel, as Bingley and Jane are now separated. The two sisters differ in their responses to the letter. Jane's good nature will not accept that Miss Bingley's motives can be anything but worthy. Elizabeth, more perceptive, suspects that malice and self-interest have driven Miss Bingley to write what is little more than wishful thinking on her part.

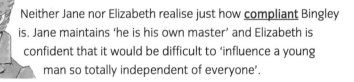

Neither Jane nor Elizabeth realise just how **compliant** Bingley is. Jane maintains 'he is his own master' and Elizabeth is confident that it would be difficult to 'influence a young man so totally independent of everyone'.

Chapter 22

> *Such was Miss Lucas's scheme.*

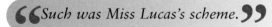

The reasons for Charlotte's acceptance of Mr Collins are purely economic. Notice Austen's irony in describing the effects of the news on the Lucas family: Sir William and Lady Lucas work out how long Mr Bennet has to live; the younger girls look forward to 'coming out'. Charlotte knows Mr Collins's faults and admits that his company is 'irksome', but in marrying him she is gaining something she prizes above happiness: financial security and comfort.

Marriage <u>'was</u> <u>the</u> <u>only</u> <u>honourable</u> <u>provision'</u> for someone in her situation, and she regards herself as lucky.

Chapter 23

> *Elizabeth felt persuaded that no real confidence could ever subsist between them again.*

Each member of the Bennet family reacts to the news of Charlotte's engagement: Mrs Bennet rants and raves; Mr Bennet is cynical; Jane wishes them well; Kitty and Lydia are uninterested in it except for its gossip value.

Mrs Bennet's obsession with getting her daughters married brings out the worst in her character. Holding Sir William and Lady Lucas responsible for their daughter's behaviour, she behaves rudely to them and, in continually reminding Jane of Bingley's absence, shows complete insensitivity for her feelings.

<u>Elizabeth</u> <u>is</u> <u>shocked</u> <u>by</u> <u>her</u> <u>friend's</u> <u>decision</u> <u>and</u> <u>fears</u> <u>losing</u> <u>their</u> <u>friendship</u>. Although they had previously discussed marriage, Elizabeth never thought Charlotte would actually accept a proposal from someone as ridiculous as Mr Collins. Her view of her friend changes as he does not believe in marrying purely for money and security. She is also worried that Bingley has not returned.

Quick quiz 1

Who? What? Where? When? Why? How?

1   Who is Mr Bennet's favourite daughter? Why?

2   Who is Mrs Bennet's favourite daughter?

3   Who is Mr Collins's patroness, and what is her other connection to events?

4   Who, according to Miss Bingley, is Mr Bingley going to marry?

5   What does Mr Darcy say to 'slight' Elizabeth at the assembly?

6   What 'discoveries' does Darcy make about Elizabeth as he becomes interested in her?

7   What warnings about Wickham are given by
(a)   Miss Bingley?
(b)   Darcy?

8   Where do the Bennets live, and what is the nearest town?

9   Why is Mrs Bennet so desperate to see her daughters married?

10   Why does Mr Collins say he wishes to marry?

11   How does Darcy feel when Elizabeth says she's leaving Netherfield?

12   How do the Bennets react to Charlotte's engagement to Mr Collins?

Who is this?

1   Who is an 'odd ... mixture of quick parts, sarcastic humour, reserve and caprice'?

2   Who is 'a woman of mean understanding, little information and uncertain temper'?

3   Who is 'good-looking and gentlemanlike', with 'easy, unaffected manners'?

Chapter 24

> **"Miss Bingley's letter arrived, and put an end to doubt."**

Jane tries, in her usual understanding way, to explain the practical issues which persuaded Charlotte to accept Mr Collins. She points out that Charlotte is **'prudent'** and the match **'eligible'**. Elizabeth takes issue with this view and with the language Jane uses: 'You shall not ... persuade yourself or me, that selfishness is prudence, and insensibility of danger, security for happiness'.

When they discuss Bingley's absence, Elizabeth is the more astute, while Jane prefers to believe that she was mistaken about Bingley's feelings, rather than accept that his sisters have persuaded him of Miss Darcy's superiority.

Chapter 25

> **"that expression of 'violently in love' is so hackneyed, so doubtful, so indefinite"**

The Gardiners represent **the sensible side of Mrs Bennet's family** and their marriage contrasts with Mr and Mrs Bennet's. In Mrs Gardiner's comment (above) is revealed Austen's condemnation of romantic love as being too fragile a basis for marriage. But sensible as she is, Mrs Gardiner is still herself subject to the pressures of her friends. Although she cannot remember Darcy's character well, she has heard that he is 'a very proud ill-natured boy'. Later, when Darcy meets the Gardiners, note the level of respect he affords them despite their coming from a 'trade' background.

Chapter 26

> **Mrs Gardiner's caution to Elizabeth was punctually and kindly given**

Jane and Charlotte, Elizabeth's closest confidantes, depart with the Gardiners and Mr Collins. The chapter is full of information by letter, and of wise advice and opinion. You will find many significant comments, among the most important of which are:

- Elizabeth's promise 'not to be in a hurry' over marriage, and her refusal to promise to be wise if tempted — together they summarise well her view of marriage

- Jane's admission to having been deceived by Miss Bingley's apparent regard

- the painless end to Elizabeth's involvement with Wickham — note what she realises about her feelings for him.

Chapter 27

> **The only pain was in leaving her father**

Notice how carefully the novel is planned. Elizabeth's mood is low and January and February pass. The relationship between Jane and Bingley seems to be over; the suspense as to whom Mr Collins will marry has gone; Wickham has lost interest in Elizabeth; general opinion of Darcy's low character is established.

Mrs Gardiner and Elizabeth discuss Wickham's motives for proposing marriage to Miss King. Elizabeth is inclined to be forgiving of him, applauding his 'rational motives': later, she condemns him as 'mercenary' — once she knows more of his character.

Chapter 28

> **❝** *the prospect of her northern tour was a constant source of delight* **❞**

Note how Austen satirises Mr Collins with his repetition of the words **'humble abode'**. Note, too, Elizabeth's sceptical assessment of the Collins household. She senses that Mr Collins is trying to show her what grand things she lost by refusing his proposal, and that Charlotte, although cheerful, ensures her own happiness by contriving to put as much distance as she can between herself and Mr Collins.

Explore

Look at Chapter 29 to see how Mr Collins does the same at Rosings.

How does Mr Collins assess the value of surroundings and nature? Everything is **quantified and numbered** rather than appreciated for its own sake. Austen mocks his lack of sensitivity to beauty: 'every view was pointed out with a minuteness which left beauty entirely behind'.

Chapter 29

> **❝** *Scarcely any thing was talked of ... but their visit to Rosings.* **❞**

Unlike the Lucases, Elizabeth is not apprehensive about meeting Lady Catherine. Elizabeth is not in awe of her, as **she attaches little importance to rank** for its own sake.

Notice how Austen uses dialogue to develop a point she has made about character. Lady Catherine's questions about Elizabeth's family are **impertinent, despite her elevated rank**. The narrator deflates Lady Catherine's claims to infallibility with: 'The party then gathered round the fire to hear Lady Catherine determine what weather they were to have on the morrow.'

Chapter 30

> **The entertainment of dining at Rosings was repeated about twice a week**

We are given more details of Lady Catherine's activities as mistress of a great estate: bossy, dictatorial and patronising, her behaviour contrasts with what we learn of Darcy's behaviour as master of Pemberley in Chapter 43.

Chapter 31

> **Colonel Fitzwilliam's manners were very much admired at the parsonage**

Notice the clever use of contrast again. Darcy was offended by the lack of breeding shown by Elizabeth's mother: now his aunt, Lady Catherine, shows her lack of manners.

Elizabeth's spirit is shown when she refuses to be intimidated by Darcy when she is playing the piano. Austen uses the formal conversation of the drawing room to imply so much more then is actually stated.
Darcy's comment: '**We neither of us perform to strangers'** shows that he appreciates Elizabeth's lack of pretence.
As members of this society, both Darcy and Elizabeth know that they are required, to some degree, to 'perform' in public. He says that shyness holds him back; she argues that practice would improve his social skills. Both are aware that **the society in which they live is formal and artificial**, and this mutual understanding is apparent beneath their polite conversation.

Chapter 32

> **Mr Darcy, and Mr Darcy only, entered the room.**

Note the way Darcy draws his chair nearer to Elizabeth, a sign of **his desire to get to know her better**. Note also his remark: 'You cannot have been always at Longbourn'. Impressed with the liveliness of Elizabeth's mind, he implies that the society found in the country cannot provide her with enough stimulus — **more evidence of his arrogance**.

Charlotte Lucas voices the reader's suspicions about Darcy's motives here, and **Austen gradually prepares us for Darcy's proposal**. Colonel Fitzwilliam's presence also increases the tension. His outgoing, agreeable personality is in contrast to Darcy's more introverted, inscrutable manner, and leads the reader to conjecture whether he is not a more suitable choice for Elizabeth.

Chapter 33

> **More than once did Elizabeth in her ramble within the Park, unexpectedly meet Mr Darcy.**

Explore

Barriers to love are as important to a romantic story as strength of attraction is. What are we to make of Elizabeth's untypically tearful reaction?

Austen creates **suspense** by making it quite clear to the reader that Darcy has fallen in love with Elizabeth, while Elizabeth remains oblivious. Fitzwilliam's function here is to provide Elizabeth with information about Darcy's part in persuading Bingley to leave Netherfield and causing her sister so much sadness.

Colonel Fitzwilliam's phrase, **'there were some very strong objections against the lady'**, causes Elizabeth a great deal of

pain. She is convinced that it is Darcy's '**pride and caprice**', his snobbery about the Bennet's 'low connections', which are the substance of the 'strong objections'. **Her pride is therefore wounded**. Be aware of the importance of 'connections' in determining a marriage. Elizabeth is convinced that it is this factor, and not their mother's lack of breeding, that chiefly convinced Darcy to persuade Bingley against a marriage with Jane.

Chapter 34

> **"In vain I have struggled."**

Austen does not use direct conversation to narrate Darcy's proposal. The narrative therefore allows her to convey Elizabeth's feelings towards his proposal while he makes it. We hear the proposal through Elizabeth.

Darcy has swallowed his pride and, in proposing to Elizabeth, **he is prepared to overlook Elizabeth's connections**, an amazing change for a man of his position in society. However, his very frankness about this only insults Elizabeth's own pride and deepens her prejudice against him. **Elizabeth's denunciation of his behaviour as ungentlemanly is cutting to someone of Darcy's status and breeding**. Note the importance of social opinion here. Elizabeth blames Darcy not merely because he has separated Bingley and her sister but also because he has exposed her sister to society's contempt. She also lays the serious charge that he deprived Wickham of advancement.

Chapter 35

> **"Be not alarmed, Madam, on receiving this letter"**

Explore

Do you find Darcy's explanations of his two supposed offences satisfactory? Was he justified in interfering in Bingley's love for Jane? Was his treatment of Wickham fair?

Darcy's letter to Elizabeth is a pivotal point in the novel. The fact that he feels the need to explain and justify his actions shows the esteem in which he holds Elizabeth. Her criticism of him has hurt his pride and, despite its formal tone, the letter shows his complete integrity. He honestly believes he has acted for the best.

Chapter 36

> **❝** *It was all pride and insolence.* **❞**

The first reading of the letter leaves Elizabeth unchanged in her prejudice and hostility against Darcy. She still cannot condone his behaviour in helping to separate Bingley and Jane. It is the story of Wickham which begins to crack the shell of Elizabeth's prejudice against Darcy. She realises that both versions cannot be true. Whose story is she to believe? Note the powerful emotions with which this realisation hits her: 'Astonishment, apprehension and even horror, oppressed her'. In her struggle to decide which of the two men is telling the truth, note how Elizabeth recognises that 'the general approbation of the neighbourhood' had formed her attitude to Wickham in the first place. With her new-found 'impartiality', she reappraises his behaviour and comes up with an entirely different view of his character.

Just as the letter has forced her to reappraise Wickham, so does it make her reconsider Darcy's character. Re-reading the first part of the letter, dealing with Bingley and Jane, she feels all his assertions to be 'just'. With great emotion she realises that she has been 'blind, partial, prejudiced, absurd'.

This is the turning-point for Elizabeth in her search for self-realisation. She blames her lack of perception on her vanity, which was flattered by Wickham's attention and offended by the impoliteness of Darcy. Putting her pride aside, she has to admit that Darcy's judgements of Jane's seeming lack of affection for Bingley and her family's gauche behaviour at the ball, are understandable.

Chapter 37

> **The two gentlemen left Rosings the next morning**

Although Elizabeth now has respect and gratitude for Darcy, she has not yet come to like him, as she still is offended by his proud manner. She also acknowledges, with bitterness, the shortcomings of her family. She accepts that it is her family's lack of breeding, rather than Darcy's overwhelming arrogance, that is the main cause of Jane's unhappiness.

Elizabeth's brief dispute with Lady Catherine, when she announces her decision to leave Rosings, finds its parallel in Chapter 56 when Elizabeth refuses to promise not to marry Darcy.

Chapter 38

> **We know how little there is to tempt any one to our humble abode.**

Mr Collins's pomposity is apparent in everything he says: his false modesty about the parsonage – 'our humble abode' – and his self-congratulation at Lady de Bourgh's patronage, are intended to underline to Elizabeth all that she has lost by not marrying him. Ironically, Elizabeth is more than aware of what she has missed: 'Poor Charlotte – it was melancholy to leave her to such society!' Although Charlotte makes the best of it, Elizabeth knows her friend can never really be happy, married to Mr Collins.

Chapter 39

❝They are going to be encamped near Brighton ❞

Lydia's main preoccupation is the soldiers at Meryton. This chapter prepares us for the next major event in the story: Lydia's elopement. All Elizabeth's fears, expressed at the end of Chapter 37, seem to be well founded: Lydia <u>is</u> <u>incapable</u> <u>of</u> <u>thinking</u> <u>seriously</u> <u>about</u> <u>anything</u>.

Chapter 40

❝She then spoke of the letter❞

Jane's reaction to the truth about the Wickham affair is typical of her nature. Incapable of believing ill of anybody, she endeavours to exonerate both Darcy and Wickham. But Elizabeth notes: <u>'One</u> <u>has</u> <u>got</u> <u>all</u> <u>the</u> <u>goodness,</u> <u>and</u> <u>the</u> <u>other</u> <u>all</u> <u>the</u> <u>appearance</u> <u>of</u> <u>it'</u>. Again the difference between appearance and reality is highlighted.

Chapter 41

❝A little sea-bathing would set me up for ever. ❞

Elizabeth <u>begins</u> <u>to</u> <u>see</u> <u>her</u> <u>family</u> <u>through</u> <u>Darcy's</u> <u>eyes</u>: the shallowness of her younger sisters, until now a source of amusement, begins to embarrass her. She can even see why Darcy persuaded Bingley against them! When Elizabeth pleads with her father not to allow Lydia to go to Brighton, he responds facetiously to her suggestion that the reputation of the whole family is at stake. Only when Elizabeth implores him to look seriously at the situation does he answer more sensibly. This scene reveals <u>Elizabeth's</u> <u>increasing</u> <u>maturity</u>, which contrasts with the irresponsibility of her father.

Explore

Observe the skill with which Elizabeth alerts Wickham to the fact that she knows the true story. She implies this without actually saying as much.

As another step towards her attachment to Darcy, Elizabeth has to untie the threads that linked her to Wickham. The fact that he thinks he can renew his attentions towards her is only offensive to her. Now she sees those attentions as 'idle and frivolous gallantry'.

Chapter 42

❝*Her father captivated by youth and beauty*❞

Mr Bennet's experience of marriage has been unhappy. <u>Austen</u> <u>warns</u> <u>against</u> <u>such</u> <u>marriages,</u> <u>based</u> <u>on</u> '<u>youth</u> <u>and</u> <u>beauty</u>' <u>and</u> <u>a</u> <u>semblance</u> <u>of</u> '<u>good</u> <u>humour</u>'. This observation is placed strategically in the novel, coming as it does before the elopement of Lydia and Wickham. This account of Mr Bennet's marriage explains his cynical and sarcastic attitude towards his family. However, Elizabeth feels that his contemptuous attitude towards his wife is a harmful example to his children. She does not think an unhappy marriage excuses his irresponsibility as a father.

Text commentary

Who? What? Where? When? Why? How?

1 Who does Mrs Collins have her eye on for Elizabeth?

2 What aspect of Darcy's proposal rouses Elizabeth to 'resentment', and what 'exasperated' her further?

3 What does Elizabeth charge Darcy with, to explain her rejection of him?

4 What bargain had Wickham made with Darcy, and how did he break it?

5 What is Elizabeth's opinion of Wickham when she sees him again?

6 Where does Jane travel to in these chapters?

7 Why is Darcy 'ill-qualified to recommend himself to strangers'?

8 Why has Charlotte chosen the least comfortable parlour for her use at Hunsford?

9 Why does Mr Bennet allow Lydia to go to Brighton?

10 How does Darcy justify his decision to separate Jane and Bingley? What does he feel bad about?

11 How does Elizabeth feel about Darcy as she leaves Hunsford to return home?

Who is this?

1 Who is 'a conceited, pompous, narrow-minded, silly man'?

2 Who is 'an amiable, intelligent, elegant woman'?

3 Who shows 'easiness of temper ... want of proper resolution'?

> **She had never seen a place for which nature had done more**

When she sees Pemberley, Elizabeth cannot help thinking that she might have been mistress of the beautiful house and park, but she quickly remembers that the Gardiners would never have been welcome there: her prejudice against Darcy's pride is still strong. Another step in changing Elizabeth's prejudiced view of Darcy is the housekeeper's account of his character and behaviour. Introduced as 'respectable-looking' and 'civil', Mrs Reynolds is clearly a woman to be believed. She interprets Darcy's 'pride' as reserve: a refusal to 'rattle away like other young men'. Elizabeth is shown Darcy's portrait, which shows him smiling!

Just as her opinion of Darcy begins to mellow, Elizabeth is brought face to face with him. Elizabeth is embarrassed in case Darcy should think she is pursuing him, but his behaviour is so different to what she expected that, ironically, it is he who puts her at ease. Her perception of the change in Darcy is the result of two factors: he has modified his proud behaviour, and Elizabeth's own feelings towards him have also changed. Pride and prejudice on both sides have been softened and altered.

Explore

Although it is not in the original text, the scene in the 1994 BBC adaptation where Colin Firth, as Mr Darcy, climbs out of the river in his undergarments encapsulates the feelings of embarrassment and awkwardness between the two characters.

Again we see the importance of 'breeding' in this society. Darcy accepts the Gardiners on the basis of their evident good breeding, despite their 'trade' background. Elizabeth is surprised at Darcy's civil manner, evident consideration for her and for her aunt and uncle, and desire for her to meet his sister.

Chapter 44

> 66 *Elizabeth had settled it that Mr Darcy would bring his sister to visit her* 99

Note the passage of time in the novel. Bingley remarks that it is more than eight months since the Netherfield ball.

On renewing Elizabeth's acquaintance, <u>Bingley</u> <u>shows</u> <u>that</u> <u>he</u> <u>still</u> <u>holds</u> <u>Jane</u> <u>in</u> <u>high</u> <u>regard</u> and regrets not having seen her for a long time. Elizabeth is heartened.

Elizabeth's analysis of her feelings at the end of this chapter is typical of <u>Austen's</u> <u>rational</u> <u>approach</u> <u>to</u> <u>love</u>. Elizabeth no longer hates or even dislikes Darcy. His good reputation and his civil manner make her respect him. The knowledge that he still loves her after her rejection of his proposal makes her grateful towards him. <u>Respect</u> <u>and</u> <u>gratitude</u> <u>are</u> <u>a</u> <u>good</u> <u>basis</u> <u>for</u> <u>marriage</u>, but she is still not sure whether marrying him would be for the best.

Chapter 45

> 66 *By Mrs Hurst and Miss Bingley, they were noticed only by a curtsey* 99

Miss Bingley's catty comment, 'Are not the —shire militia removed from Meryton? They must be a great loss to your family', backfires on her: she does not know the story about Wickham and Miss Darcy's elopement. Intending to unnerve Elizabeth, she causes pain to the Darcys. This chapter is a fine study of <u>Miss</u> <u>Bingley's</u> <u>jealousy</u> which 'gave no one any pain but herself'.

Chapter 46

> 66 *So imprudent a match on both sides!* 99

Just as there seemed a real chance that the relationship between Elizabeth and Darcy could prosper, news of Lydia's elopement arrives. <u>It is important that Darcy is present when Elizabeth receives the news</u>. He sees her distress and it is he who will later arrange the marriage and provide the finance for the wedding settlement. Ironically, Elizabeth regrets telling him of the family's disgrace, fearing that she has lost her chance with him forever: her final misjudgement of his character.

Chapter 47

> 66 *Wickham will never marry a woman with out some money.* 99

Elizabeth is <u>**worried about Wickham's intentions,**</u> and is doubtful that marriage to Lydia is in his plans. Under no delusions about Wickham's character, and knowing about his attempted elopement with Georgiana Darcy, Elizabeth has no choice but to see the reality of the situation. She <u>blames herself</u> for Lydia's predicament because she did not make known to her parents what she knew of Wickham's character. Mrs Bennet refuses to accept any personal responsibility for what has happened.

Explore

Social etiquette means that Lydia's elopement will almost certainly prevent the other sisters from marrying. However, despite this Mrs Bennet attributes none of the blame to Lydia. Why is this?

The reader has followed Elizabeth's travels and thus comes upon the other Bennets in the midst of their attempts to deal with the problem. Once again they are presented in a far from flattering light, and Elizabeth is moved to words and gestures of incredulity at the self-obsession of her mother and sisters, with the notable exception of Jane.

Chapter 48

> 66 *Every body declared he was the wickedest young man in the world* 99

Mr Collins's letter speaks of his <u>relief</u> at not having married into the family. Selfish and sanctimonious as ever, his 'Christianity' is shown to be shallow when he recommends that Mr Bennet 'throw off the unworthy child from your affection for ever'.

Mr Bennet now acknowledges that he has <u>not taken his paternal duties seriously enough</u>. He admits to Elizabeth that he should have taken her advice and refused to let Lydia go to Brighton. <u>Note It is only Mr Gardiner who actually does anything</u>.

Chapter 49

> **❝** *there is an express come for master from Mr Gardiner* **❞**

Money played an important part in marriage. Mr Bennet and Elizabeth agree that Mr Wickham would not have agreed to marry for less than <u>£10,000: a vast sum in those days</u>. It is essential that Lydia and Wickham should marry. Even though their chance of happiness is small and Wickham is disliked, the public disgrace of elopement without marriage was very great and would have reflected on the whole Bennet family (as shown by Mr Collins's letter).

Mrs Bennet thinks only of the joy of having one daughter married, regardless of the scandalous circumstances. Note her ingratitude on hearing that Mr Gardiner has given Wickham money as part of the marriage settlement.

Elizabeth's wisdom is apparent again here. In contrast to the inane prattling of her mother, <u>Elizabeth assesses Lydia's situation rationally</u> and concludes that, while by no means ideal (for she does not rate her chances of 'rational happiness or worldly prosperity' very highly), it is considerably better than it had been before.

Chapter 50

> **When first Mr Bennet had married, economy was held to be perfectly useless**

Mr Bennet is ashamed that his brother-in-law has had to bear the expense of Lydia's marriage settlement, but glad not to have been put to too much trouble by the affair. We learn that his irresponsibility towards his daughters extends to financial matters: <u>he has not saved any money to support his family after his death</u>.

Austen mocks the public response to the wedding, criticising the hypocrisy of the 'spiteful old ladies of Meryton' who, knowing Wickham's character, and knowing there is little chance of Lydia being happy, send 'good-natured wishes for her well-doing'.

Elizabeth now recognises that she loves Darcy, and that their marriage <u>'must have been to the advantage of both'</u>. The irony is that she knows a man of his status will not wish to be associated with her family after such a scandal. <u>Here, Austen describes an 'ideal' marriage, based on mutual suitability</u>. Elizabeth would have benefited from Darcy's 'knowledge of the world', Darcy from her 'ease and liveliness'. This rational approach to marriage contrasts with Lydia and Wickham's: the latter is a marriage that Elizabeth is convinced will not work because 'passions were stronger than virtue'.

Chapter 51

> **Lydia was Lydia still; untamed, unabashed, wild, noisy, and fearless.**

Elizabeth, imagining how she would feel in Lydia's position, looks for signs of shame and embarrassment when Lydia returns to

Longbourn. She is shocked to find no such signs. However, Wickham has the grace to look shamefaced. Lydia's insensitivity to the feelings and efforts of those who brought about her 'honourable' marriage is apparent in her attitude that it would be 'fun' to be married. <u>Her behaviour</u> <u>is</u> <u>as</u> <u>thoughtless</u> <u>and</u> <u>insensitive</u> <u>as</u> <u>her mother's</u>. Look at the way she lets William Goulding know she is married, and the way she speaks to Jane when the family goes to dinner.

Chapter 52

> **❝He had done all this for a girl he could neither regard nor esteem.❞**

The letter from Mrs Gardiner describes how far the Bennet family are <u>indebted</u> <u>to</u> <u>Darcy</u>. Elizabeth, conscious that Darcy's actions were prompted by his feelings for her, regrets all the 'saucy speech' and 'every ungracious sensation' she has ever directed towards him. She admits her love for him and is proud of the way he has acted. But she is still convinced that he would never tolerate Wickham as a brother-in-law.

In a very subtle and ironic way, Elizabeth lets Wickham know that she has been told about his past. Wickham asks leading questions, but is not happy with her answers — although you should note that he offers no denial of Mrs Reynolds' story. Note, too, the irony with which Elizabeth suggests that she knows about Wickham's planned elopement with Darcy's sister, saying that Miss Darcy 'has got over the most trying age'.

Chapter 53

> **❝The day of his and Lydia's departure soon came❞**

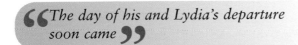

In her usual inconsiderate, insensitive way, Mrs Bennet rattles on about Bingley's arrival (having first said she will not talk about it), with no consideration for Jane's feelings. The arrival of the two men at Longbourn makes for an awkward meeting. Darcy seems to have **reverted to his former manner, distant, and 'serious as usual'**. Elizabeth attributes his thoughtful and silent behaviour to his dislike of her mother's company. To Elizabeth's embarrassment, Mrs Bennet dwells at length on Lydia's wedding to Wickham, whose name is an embarrassment to both Elizabeth and Darcy.

Elizabeth is filled with despair by her mother's insensitivity. Even if Bingley and Darcy are fond of Jane and herself, her mother's lack of breeding and Lydia's scandal must stand in the way of their happiness. However, she is given cause to hope that Bingley retains affection for Jane, as he renews his attentions.

Chapter 54

66 *Mr Darcy's behaviour astonished and vexed her.* **99**

The suspense about Elizabeth's and Darcy's relationship is prolonged by **Darcy's quiet, distant behaviour**, and Elizabeth does not have the opportunity of speaking more than a few words with him. However, everyone except Jane is sure of Bingley's affection for her. Elizabeth thinks Jane is not being honest with herself.

Chapter 55

66 *Oh! why is not every body as happy.* **99**

The way Mrs Bennet engineers the situation so that Jane and Bingley are left alone together is comic, and does not have the desired outcome — initially. However, after seeing her father in

the proper manner, Bingley proposes to Jane. **Austen's ideal of marriage** is again set out here. Happiness is **'rationally founded'**, and the marriage is likely to be a success because of the **'excellent understanding'** and general similarity of feeling and taste between the two. Mr Bennet's prediction that they will be cheated by their servants and forever spending beyond their means is a comic reflection on the generosity of the couple.

Explore

We see two sides of Elizabeth's independence in rapid succession: her resilience and humour in Chapter 55, followed by her remarkable resistance to Lady Catherine in Chapter 56.

Note Elizabeth's resilience of character here: even though she is despondent about her chances of marrying Darcy, **she is genuinely happy for her sister**, and even makes light of her own single state: 'if I have very good luck, I may meet with another Mr Collins in time'.

Chapter 56

> **It was Lady Catherine de Bourgh.**

Notice the scathing way in which Lady de Bourgh criticises the house and garden at Longbourn and how Mrs Bennet, overwhelmed by being in the presence of a lady, is civil for once. When she and Elizabeth are alone, Lady Catherine abruptly introduces the subject of Elizabeth's engagement to Mr Darcy. Elizabeth, refusing to be intimidated by rank and already annoyed by Lady Catherine's offensive manner, refuses to answer her questions directly. If Lady Catherine had been less obnoxious, perhaps Elizabeth would have been more open. Elizabeth's defiance shocks Lady Catherine, who makes plain her reasons for opposing a marriage between Darcy and Elizabeth: **'honour, decorum, prudence, nay, interest, forbid it'** — all reasons which Darcy had declared he had overcome when he proposed to Elizabeth at Hunsford.

Elizabeth's **intelligence** comes through in the way she argues with Lady Catherine, turning all her accusations back to their source: 'Your ladyship had declared it to be impossible'. Notice the **dignity** with which she responds to this interfering woman, who does her best to intimidate her. When Lady Catherine, in desperation, reminds Elizabeth of Lydia's scandal, Elizabeth musters all her dignity and cuts the conversation dead. It is Elizabeth, not Lady Catherine, who brings the interview to a close.

Chapter 57

> **❝** *I did not know before, that I had two daughters on the brink of matrimony.* **❞**

The **suspense** about Elizabeth's and Darcy's relationship is maintained. Still unsure of his feelings, and more upset by the interview with Lady Catherine than she showed, Elizabeth is convinced she must have lost Darcy for ever. The letter from Mr Collins only causes Elizabeth pain because she is forced to laugh with her father at the preposterous rumour about her engagement. Mr Bennet's sense of the absurd is roused by the suggestion that Darcy is interested in Elizabeth, for he thinks that she loathes him. He does not realise how hurtful he is being to his daughter as he unwittingly hits on the truth: 'did she [Lady Catherine] call to refuse her consent?'.

Chapter 58

> **❝** *You are too generous to trifle with me.* **❞**

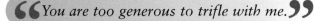

Look at the way Austen handles Darcy's declaration of love. There is **no** **physical** **contact** between the lovers: Elizabeth does not even meet his eye while he declares his love. This is **a** **rational** **union** based on mutual suitability of mind, rather than physical passion.

Both of them go back over the past year of their acquaintance, reliving the obstacles which they had to overcome: pride and prejudice on both sides. Each has been 'humbled' by the other, and both feel that they are to blame.

Ironically, it is Lady Catherine they have to thank for bringing them together at the end — Darcy says Elizabeth's refusal to deny their engagement 'taught [him] to hope'.

Although they have resolved all their difficulties, Elizabeth is sensitive enough to appreciate that their relationship still needs to develop. Though she realises that her witty, spirited repartee will make a good foil to his serious nature, she knows that he is not yet ready to be teased. It is important to note that the narrator never reveals the conversation that takes place between Elizabeth and Darcy when they finally declare their love to one another.

Chapter 59

❝*He still loves me, and we are engaged.***❞**

Elizabeth is understandably uneasy about her family's reaction to the news of her engagement. Note again the emphasis on **controlling** **feelings** **by** **rational** **means**.

Jane and Mr Bennet are astonished by the news, as they were both so sure that Elizabeth heartily disliked Darcy. Her father is touchingly worried that Elizabeth does not love Darcy and she puts his mind at rest on that score. Mrs Bennet's reaction is fulsome indeed, and she conveniently forgets how much she dislikes Darcy, in her excitement at Elizabeth's wealthy match.

Chapter 60

> ❝*I cannot fix on the hour, or the spot,
> or the look or the words* ❞

The marriage of Darcy and Elizabeth is so unlikely an outcome after their first meetings that they several times (Chapter 58 is another example) review and re-interpret earlier events. Here, Elizabeth asks Darcy to account for falling in love with her. You will find it of value and interest to re-read key events with later explanations in mind.

Chapter 61

> ❝*Happy for all her maternal feelings was
> the day on which Mrs Bennet got rid of
> her two most deserving daughters.*❞

All the threads of the novel are tidily drawn together. Jane and Bingley move to Derbyshire after a year at Netherfield. Kitty's character improves without the presence of Lydia and under the influence of her elder sisters. Mary, though still inclined to moralise, becomes more sociable now that she is no longer in the shadow of her more gifted elder sisters. As predicted, Wickham and Lydia's marriage turns sour and they are continually in debt.

Explore

There is a famous Oscar Wilde quotation: 'The good ended happily, and the bad unhappily. That is what Fiction means.' Is that true of *Pride and Prejudice*?

Many eighteenth- and nineteenth-century novels end with a brief summary of the future lives of the main characters. Thus, rather than a dramatic, comic or romantic conclusion, Austen leaves us with the continuing happiness of the Gardiners, though the last words refer to the marriage of Elizabeth and Darcy. What happens to the characters after the novel finishes? Is it a happy ending?

Who? What? Where? When? Why? How?

1   Who is assumed to have paid Wickham to marry Lydia? Why is this ironic?

2   Who does Darcy bring to visit Elizabeth at Lambton, and with what effect?

3   What factors, encountered at Pemberley, put Darcy in a different light?

4   What opposite extremes do Mr and Mrs Bennet adopt in reaction to Lydia's impending marriage?

5   What prompts Mr Darcy's second proposal?

6   What does Elizabeth refuse to give Lady Catherine?

7   Where do Elizabeth's private conversations with Lady Catherine and Darcy take place?

8   Why, according to Elizabeth, did Darcy first fall in love with her?

9   Why had Wickham left the regiment, and what were his plans with regard to Lydia?

10   How does Elizabeth misjudge Darcy's character, even after she realises she loves him?

11   How does Elizabeth reprove Wickham this time?

12   How does Mrs Bennet react to Jane's engagement? And Elizabeth's?

Who is this?

1   Who is 'as false and deceitful as he is insinuating'?

2   Who 'was always the sweetest-tempered, most generous-hearted boy in the world'?

3   Who says, 'I have not been in the habit of brooking disappointment'?

Writing essays

- The first essential requirement is thorough revision. You will have time to look up quotations and references, but only if you know where to look.

- Read the questions carefully, making sure you underline key words that tell you what to do, e.g 'compare', 'contrast', 'explore', 'explain'. Retelling the story will get you no credit.

- Jot down the main points, **make an essay plan** that shows what you are going to include in each paragraph, then stick to it (see page 72). Make sure you link the paragraphs to each other and refer back to the question to avoid digressing.

- Summarise in your introduction how you plan to approach the question, then jump straight into your argument. Ensure you answer *all* of the question not just part of it.

- Take care with spelling, punctuation and grammar. Avoid using slang or abbreviations. Write in paragraphs, starting a new line and indenting quotations of more than a few words. Quotations should be used to increase the clarity of your answer, but extended quotations (more than a few sentences) are usually unhelpful.

- It is important to back up what you say. Remember: **point–quotation–comment** (see page 68). This will ensure that your work stays analytical.

- Finally, use your conclusion to sum up your points and relate them back to the question. If you have missed something, put it in now. Leave five minutes to proofread your work for mistakes.

- Some of you are probably studying *Pride and Prejudice* as part of a Wide Reading coursework assignment for GCSE English/English Literature. The requirement of the AQA examination board is that this assignment must involve comparison between a complete pre-twentieth-century prose text and a suitable twentieth-century text. It is also essential to make certain comments on the historical, social and cultural background to the texts. Jane Austen's novels are particularly suitable in this respect: her presentation of the manners, morals and attitudes of the early nineteenth century is crucial to the success of her fiction. Alternatively, you may be writing about the novel as a piece of pre-twentieth-century coursework as part of the Edexcel syllabus.

- It is **essential** to make reference to the social and cultural background. The society inhabited by Austen's characters is of key importance.

- You should develop an argument, avoiding becoming too narrative. **Make an essay plan** and stick to it (see page 72). Refer back to the question while writing the essay to avoid digressing. When writing a comparative piece, the comparison should be made throughout the essay, not just at the end.

- Take advantage of being able to draft your essay so that the neat copy is as polished as possible.

- As with examination essays, quote from the text to support your points and make sure your conclusion summarises your arguments. Only at this stage can you consider giving your opinion. The main body of the essay should not contain personal pronouns. Again, don't forget to proofread.

- Essays will generally be expected to be 1000–1500 words in length, but follow the advice of your teacher.

Key quotations

The following are examples of **points, quotations and comments** that could be used in an essay on *Pride and Prejudice*.

1 Jane Austen's satirical view of the 'marriage market' can be seen in the opening lines of the novel:

> **❝** *It is a truth universally acknowledged, that a single man in possession of a good fortune, must be in want of a wife.* **❞** *(Chapter 1)*

This is a deliberately dramatic overstatement. It indicates both that 'the truth' is somewhat different to that presented and that this version of the truth (and the society that universally acknowledges it) is laughable.

2 Mrs Bennet is shown by the narrator to be a foolish and narrow-minded scheming woman. When Jane is invited to Netherfield, she will not allow her to use the carriage. It rains and Jane is taken ill:

> **❝** *Oh! I am not at all afraid of her dying. People do not die of trifling little colds. She will be taken good care of. As long as she stays there, it is all very well.* **❞** *(Chapter 7)*

Mrs Bennet is unconcerned about Jane's health. She simply sees an opportunity for Jane to ingratiate herself more with the Bingleys. As a result of her scheme she hopes Jane will marry Bingley and look after her, as Bingley is a wealthy man.

3 Darcy's pride is first shown when he attends the ball where he meets Elizabeth Bennet. He slights her when his friend Bingley suggests he ask her to dance. He says:

> **She is tolerable; but not handsome enough to tempt me; and I am in no humour to give consequence to young ladies who are slighted by other men.**
> *(Chapter 3)*

This thoughtless and proud comment causes Elizabeth to take an instant dislike to Darcy as he has wounded her pride. Her prejudice from this point clouds her judgement of Darcy's and Wickham's true characters.

4 The narrator shows how unsuccessful Lydia and Wickham's marriage will be:

> **Wickham's affection for Lydia, was just what Elizabeth had expected to find it; not equal to Lydia's for him.** *(Chapter 51)*

This shows that their marriage is not an equal one or a meeting of minds, but is based on Lydia's passion and a healthy financial settlement.

Key quotations

1. Pride and Prejudice *has been described as 'one of the most perfect, most pleasurable and most subtle ... of romantic love stories.' What similarities and differences do you see between Jane Austen's treatment of the traditions of romance and that of Daphne du Maurier in* Rebecca?

2. *Jane Austen's depiction of the gentry and minor nobility in* Pride and Prejudice *not only satirises the conventions of her day, but also eternal human failings and vanities. Compare her satirical targets and methods with a twentieth-century satire on the middle classes, E. M. Delafield's* Diary of a Provincial Lady.

3. *Explore how the events of the novel change Darcy's pride and Elizabeth's prejudice.*

4. *How does Jane Austen use letters both to reveal character and to progress the storyline?*

5. *'Marriage then, ideally is a love-match, and still ideally, more is involved — the character and fortune of the lover.' To what extent do the marriages in* Pride and Prejudice *fulfil Jane Austen's view of an ideal marriage?*

6. *Are there any true villains in Jane Austen's* Pride and Prejudice?

7. *How far is the title* Pride and Prejudice *appropriate to this novel? You should consider which characters show pride and/or prejudice, how their conduct and attitudes change during the novel, and the extent to which Austen reveals her own opinions on the subject.*

8. *Compare the small-town narrow-mindedness in* Pride and Prejudice *with the more lethal form in Harper Lee's* To Kill A Mockingbird.

9. *Elizabeth Bennet is a famously independent-minded heroine. How does Jane Austen's presentation of her compare with the intelligent and troubled women in the stories of Margaret Atwood?*

10. *How does Austen demonstrate through the narrator what she considers to be socially acceptable behaviour?*

11. *How does Jane Austen use humour to demonstrate character in* Pride and Prejudice?

12. *Compare the attitudes towards marriage of two different characters in the novel. Does Austen try to dictate to the reader what an ideal marriage would be?*

13. *To what extent could* Pride and Prejudice *be said to have a happy ending?*

14. *Mr Darcy is perfectly civil towards the Gardiners despite Elizabeth's fears that he would dislike them due to their inferior social background. Explore Mr Darcy's views on class and etiquette in* Pride and Prejudice.

15. *Examine the importance of social class and assess whether there was any possibility of class mobility in Jane Austen's* Pride and Prejudice.

16. *Compare the relationship of Jane and Bingley with that of Elizabeth and Darcy. Which is more likely, in Austen's eyes, to be a more successful marriage?*

17. *Compare and contrast the three main male characters, Darcy, Bingley and Wickham.*

18. *How does Austen use satirical wit to make the reader aware of her views of Mrs Bennet, Mr Collins and Lady Catherine de Bourgh?*

19. *Which title do you think best suits the novel,* Pride and Prejudice *or its original title* First Impressions? *Please refer closely to the text.*

20. *'Single Women have a dreadful propensity for being poor — which is one very strong argument in favour of matrimony.' To what extent does this statement encapsulate Jane Austen's view of the plight of the single woman?*

Planning an essay

There are several ways of planning an essay either for coursework or as part of an examination. One of the quickest, simplest and easiest to follow is the spidergram. Creating a spidergram is easy, just complete the following steps.

- Put the key words of the essay question in the centre of your map and work outwards from this.

- Make sure you use different colours if the essay asks you to look at either different characters or different themes. This will make them easy to isolate at a glance.

- Draw lines out from the centre that relate directly to the question. From these lines, draw further lines and write anything specifically related to this area of the question.

- Remember, only have one idea at the end of each line or your drawing may become confusing.

The next few pages show you how you could use spidergrams to plan the answers to three of the sample essay questions.

If you find that using spidergrams is not for you, don't panic, there are other ways of planning your answers.

- You can underline the key words in the title to ensure that you understand the focus of the essay.

- Then write down in bullet points what will be included in each paragraph from the introduction to the conclusion.

- Next, try to find relevant quotations to support your points and either write down the quotation or page reference so that it can be easily found.

Ensure that you stick to your plan and refer back to the question so as not to digress from it.

In an examination, always hand in any plan that you have written as you may be given some credit for it if you are unable to complete the full essay.

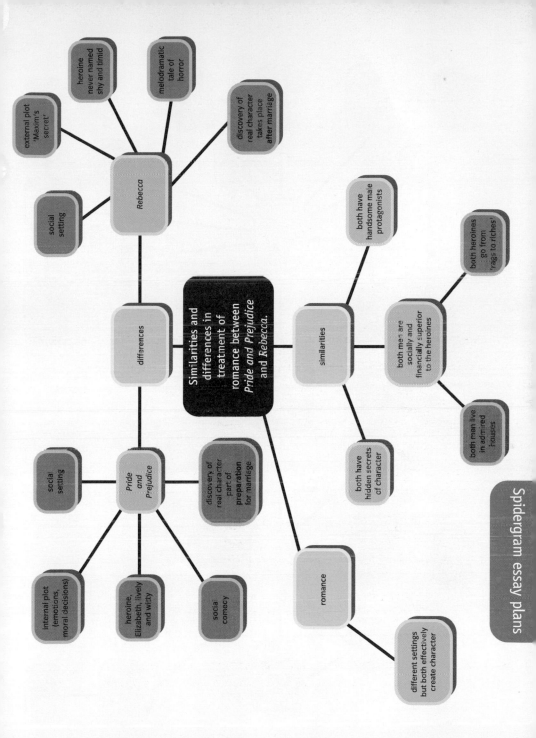

Similarities and differences in treatment of romance between *Pride and Prejudice* and *Rebecca*.

differences

Rebecca
- external plot 'Maxim's secret'
- heroine never named shy and timid
- melodramatic tale of horror
- discovery of real character takes place after marriage
- social setting

Pride and Prejudice
- social setting
- internal plot (emotions, moral decisions)
- heroine, Elizabeth, lively and witty
- social comedy
- discovery of real character part of preparation for marriage

similarities
- both have handsome male protagonists
- both men are socially and financially superior to the heroines
  - both heroines go from 'rags to riches'
  - both men live in admired houses
- both have hidden secrets of character

romance
- different settings but both effectively create character

Spidergram essay plans

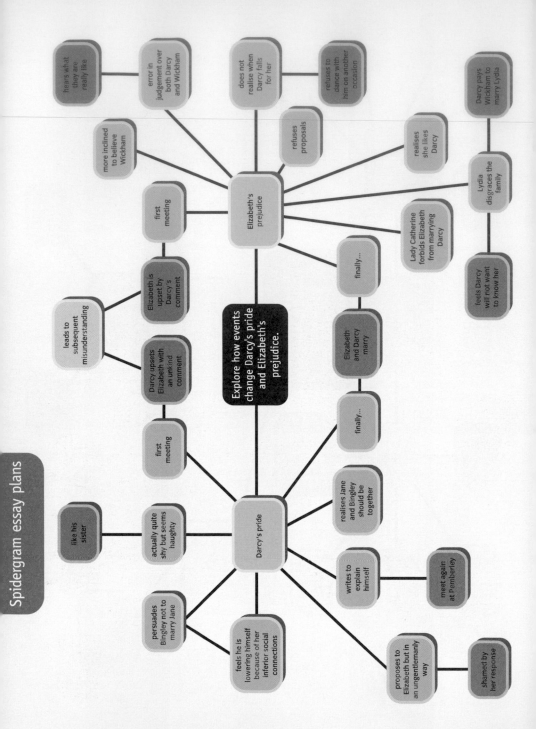

Explore how events change Darcy's pride and Elizabeth's prejudice.

Elizabeth's prejudice
- first meeting
  - error in judgement over both Darcy and Wickham
    - hears what they are really like
- more inclined to believe Wickham
- refuses proposals
- does not realise when Darcy falls for her
  - refuses to dance with him on another occasion
- realises she likes Darcy
- Lady Catherine forbids Elizabeth from marrying Darcy
- Lydia disgraces the family
  - Darcy pays Wickham to marry Lydia
  - feels Darcy will not want to know her
- finally...

Elizabeth is upset by Darcy's comment
- leads to subsequent misunderstanding

Darcy upsets Elizabeth with an unkind comment
- first meeting

Darcy's pride
- actually quite shy but seems haughty
  - like his sister
- persuades Bingley not to marry Jane
- feels he is lowering himself because of her inferior social connections
- proposes to Elizabeth but in an ungentlemanly way
  - shamed by her response
- writes to explain himself
  - meet again at Pemberley
- realises Jane and Bingley should be together
- finally...

Elizabeth and Darcy marry

74

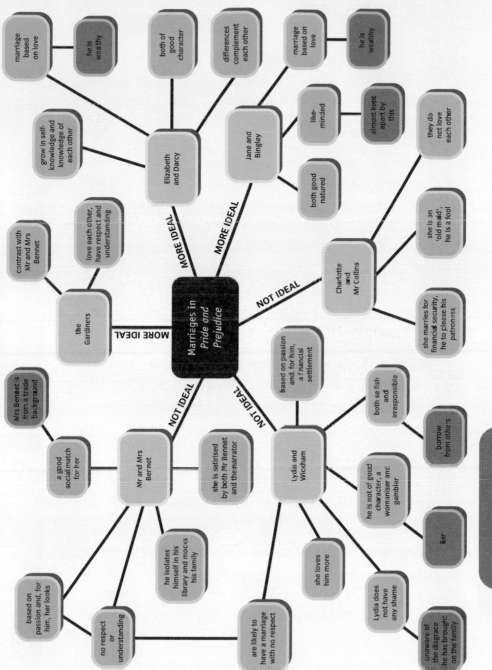

Marriages in *Pride and Prejudice*

MORE IDEAL

Elizabeth and Darcy
- marriage based on love
  - he is wealthy
- both of good character
- differences complement each other
- grow in self-knowledge and knowledge of each other

MORE IDEAL

Jane and Bingley
- marriage based on love
  - he is wealthy
- like-minded
  - almost kept apart by this
- both good natured

MORE IDEAL

the Gardiners
- contrast with Mr and Mrs Bennet
- love each other, have respect and understanding

NOT IDEAL

Charlotte and Mr Collins
- they do not love each other
- she is an 'old maid', he is a fool
- she marries for financial security, he to please his patroness

NOT IDEAL

Mr and Mrs Bennet
- Mrs Bennet is from a trade background
- a good social match for her
- she is satirised by both Mr Bennet and the narrator
- he isolates himself in his library and mocks his family
- based on passion and, for him, her looks
- no respect or understanding
- are likely to have a marriage with no respect

NOT IDEAL

Lydia and Wickham
- based on passion and, for him, a financial settlement
- both selfish and irresponsible
- borrow from others
- he is not of good character, a womaniser and gambler
- liar
- she loves him more
- Lydia does not have any shame
- unaware of the disgrace he has brought on the family

Sample response

'Marriage then, ideally is a love-match, and still ideally, more is involved — the character and fortune of the lover.' To what extent do the marriages in *Pride and Prejudice* fulfil Jane Austen's views on an ideal marriage?

'Pride and Prejudice' is one of Jane Austen's most famous novels about marriage. ✔ There are marriages that look as though they will be successful and some that seem doomed to failure. The successful marriages are those that have financial security, people of good character and love. ✔ Austen makes it clear that these marriages are those of Jane and Bingley, Elizabeth and Darcy and the Gardiners. Mr and Mrs Bennet, Charlotte Lucas and Mr Collins and Lydia and Wickham's marriages do not have all of these qualities. ✔

Jane and Bingley have a marriage based on love. They are similar characters and are loved by those around them. She is the handsomest of the Bennet sisters and is seen by all to be good-humoured, kind and gentle. ✔ Both Bingley and Jane are willing to believe the best about people and Elizabeth warns Jane about this:

'Oh! You are a great deal too apt you know, to like people in general. You never see a fault in anybody.'

Both are naïve about the motives of others and nearly do not get together because Jane does not show Bingley she likes him and he only marries her after Darcy gives his consent to their marriage. Although he likes her, he values his friend's opinion over his own. ✔

Their marriage does fulfil the ideal marriage as they are in love, he is wealthy and they are both nice people who have the same ideas about life.

Elizabeth and Darcy also have many aspects of Austen's ideal marriage. He is wealthy and they fall in love when they know themselves and each other better than they did at the start. ✔
To begin with they do not get on, he thinks she is not that attractive and she thinks he is rude and proud. He describes her as:

'tolerable; but not handsome enough to tempt me; and I am in no humour to give consequence to young ladies who are slighted by other men.'

She is offended by this and resolves to hate him as he has no manners. This leads her to misjudge both him and Wickham later in the novel. It is only when they have overcome their pride and prejudice that they realise how much they like each other. ✔

This marriage also has elements that make up a good marriage as, although they are not alike, their differences complement each other and their life will certainly never be boring. He has wealth and they are both decent people. Jane Austen would see this as a successful marriage. ✔

The other marriage that goes some way towards being ideal from Austen's point of view is that of the Gardiners. Mr Gardiner is Mrs Bennet's brother and has every good quality that she does not. He loves his wife, he works hard, and although he is not rich he makes a good living. It is the Gardiners who eventually bring Elizabeth and Darcy together. ✔ They are shown to be the opposite to Mr and Mrs Bennet, who Austen shows to have nothing in common and no respect in their marriage. ✔

In conclusion, Jane Austen shows her ideals about marriage fulfilled by the three marriages mentioned above as they are based on love, respect and financial security. Mr and Mrs Bennet do not have this and neither do Lydia and Wickham. These marriages lack respect and understanding. Passion alone will not make a marriage last. Neither will money. Charlotte Lucas and Wickham both marry their partners for a financial settlement which is not ideal either. Austen shows that these marriages that are less ideal stand little chance of being happy in the long term. All her characters, you get the feeling, will reap what they sow. ✔

Examiner's comments

The candidate shows a good understanding of what Austen thinks makes an 'ideal' marriage and which marriages fulfil this. However, this essay does not really look at the less 'ideal' marriages in sufficient detail — they are just squeezed into the conclusion. Another point to consider is how Austen uses her satirical narrator to guide the reader's opinions of both the characters and the marriages within the novel. More direct references to text would also have enhanced this essay.

Sample response

'Marriage then, ideally is a love-match, and still ideally, more is involved — the character and fortune of the lover.' To what extent do the marriages in *Pride and Prejudice* fulfil Jane Austen's views on an ideal marriage?

Marriage is a prominent theme in Jane Austen novels and particularly in 'Pride and Prejudice'. ✔ The novel is primarily concerned with the young female characters making a 'good match'. ✔ Four marriages take place during the course of the novel and the reader is encouraged to develop opinions about how 'successful' these are likely to be in the long term. ✔

Throughout the novel, the reader is guided by the views and perspective of the omniscient narrator who makes judgements about the characters and their partnerships. ✔ By the end of the novel the reader is left in no doubt as to which characters' marriages would be highly regarded by Austen and which are not founded on respect, financial security and, of course, love. ✔

The first marriage that the reader is exposed to is already in existence at the start of the novel, that of Mr and Mrs Bennet. Immediately it becomes apparent that this is not an ideal marriage as there is no respect or understanding between those involved. ✔ The narrator describes how incompatible they are in no uncertain terms:

'Mr Bennet was so odd a mixture of quick parts, sarcastic humour, reserve and caprice, that the experience of three and twenty years had been insufficient to make his wife understand his character ... She was a woman of mean understanding, little information, and uncertain temper.'

This clearly demonstrates that despite the amount of time they have been married there is still no mutual understanding or similarity between their characters. They are as different as night is from day. ✔ Their marriage cannot in any way be seen to be ideal. She has neither the intelligence nor the inclination to understand him, and he in return prefers to mock her foolish behaviour or retire to his library. Their relationship is not based on love, contains little or no affection and their views differ on virtually everything. She considers it vital that her daughters marry wealthy young men, he has realised through his own marriage that there are other considerations that are far more important. ✔ The narrator explains how Mr Bennet,

'captivated by youth and beauty, and that appearance of good humour, which youth and beauty generally give, had married a woman whose weak understanding and illiberal mind, had very early in their marriage put an end to all real affection for her.'

Their marriage had been based on his initial passion for her and her wanting to marry a gentleman as she came from a 'trade background'. This is clearly not a good basis for marriage. ✔ They do not even agree on whether Elizabeth should marry the ridiculous, yet financially secure Mr Collins and are not united in their roles as parents.

When he realises that Elizabeth intends to marry Darcy, Mr Bennet demonstrates his knowledge of his own situation and warns Elizabeth about the pitfalls of marrying someone for the 'wrong' reasons. ✔ He says:

'My child, let me not have the grief of seeing you unable to respect your partner in life.'

He does not want Elizabeth to endure the same misery and suffering as he has sentenced himself to through his marriage. ✔ Mr Bennet has learnt the true meaning of the expression 'marry in haste, repent at leisure'.

Passion is consistently shown by Jane Austen to be a foolish basis for marriage and never more so than in the union between Lydia and Wickham. Lydia is her mother's favourite child and can do no wrong, even when she elopes with a scoundrel like Wickham. It seems ironic that despite seeing her parents' loveless relationship Lydia is going to be subjected to the same fate. Neither she nor her husband are of 'good character' and he has to be paid by Darcy to marry her. They have neither financial security, love or respect. It is an unequal union, with her feelings for him being by far the stronger. ✔ The narrator explains:

'Wickham's affection for Lydia, was just what Elizabeth had expected to find it; not equal to hers for him.'

This marriage cannot be a success as it is not in any way an equal partnership, they have neither understanding, financial security, or love. ✔ Austen explains how they rely on Jane and Bingley and Elizabeth and Darcy's generosity as neither are capable of taking on responsibility. Austen also cites how eventually they become indifferent to one another. ✔

Just as Austen does not believe in marriage based purely on passion, it is equally apparent that marrying purely for financial reasons is also something to be condemned. This is shown not only through Wickham marrying Lydia but also the marriage of Charlotte Lucas to Mr Collins. Charlotte is in an unfortunate situation, she has neither beauty nor money to commend her and has reached the age of 27 and is still unmarried. Her decision to marry Mr Collins is pragmatic rather than emotional as she seeks only security and a stable future. ✔ Elizabeth is shocked when she marries Mr Collins and feels that this decision has forever affected their friendship. Charlotte explains that she has never sought romance, and that she believes:

'Happiness in marriage is entirely a matter of chance ... it is better to know as little as possible of the defects of the person with whom you are to pass your life.'

The narrator makes it clear that Charlotte will have a lifetime to consider the consequences of such a marriage. However, when Elizabeth visits, Charlotte seems content and has altered her home so that she sees as little of her husband as possible. The satirical descriptions of Mr Collins's ridiculous character and fawning behaviour towards his patroness, leave the reader with no illusions about this marriage. ✔ The two characters involved barely know each other and are by no means like-minded in their views. ✔

The importance of being both of 'good character', having shared views, financial security and respect for the other is extremely important in a marriage. This is demonstrated through the relationship between Jane and Bingley. He is a wealthy young man who is immediately attracted to Jane:

'she is the most beautiful creature I ever beheld.' ✔

They are drawn to each other from the beginning and are both 'sweet natured' caring individuals who always see the good in people. This seems like an absolutely ideal marriage but it is these qualities that almost keep them apart. ✔ Both are too trusting and not cynical enough about the motives of others. Her unwillingness to make her feelings for him known, coupled with the interference of others, almost prevents their union. ✔ Mr Bennet summarises their situation by saying:

'You are each of you so complying, that nothing will ever be resolved on; so easy, that every servant will cheat you; and so generous, that you will always exceed your income.'

The marriage of Jane and Bingley in many ways fulfils Austen's ideals about marriage, but this is still not a perfect marriage. Both characters are so compliant that there is no real spirit or fire in their relationship. Perhaps in some ways they are too similar. ✔

Elizabeth and Darcy's marriage, like Jane and Bingley's is again fairly close to fulfilling Jane Austen's views on an ideal marriage. ✔ He is a man of fortune, they are both of 'good character' and like Jane and Bingley, they marry for love. Perhaps what sets their relationship apart from the others in the novel is that they alone really progress as characters and develop their relationship. They begin at loggerheads and allow their pride and prejudice to cloud their judgement of each other. After an unfortunate first meeting, Elizabeth decides that she intensely dislikes Darcy, and later when he proposes to her, in spite of the fact that her 'condition in life' is so decidedly beneath his own, she makes her feelings clear:

'I had not known you a month before I felt you were the last man in the world whom I could ever be prevailed on to marry.'

Her fury at his attitude and ungentlemanly behaviour prevents her from seeing his true character. It is only through both characters growing in self-knowledge and knowledge of each other that their union is made possible. ✔

As the novel progresses it becomes obvious that they are suited and that their differences complement each other. He admires her lively wit and she becomes aware that his haughty behaviour masks his shyness in social situations. They grow as characters and are eventually united in marriage. ✔ Elizabeth jests with Jane about the way her feelings for Darcy have gradually developed. She confides:

'It has been coming on so gradually, that I hardly remember when it began. But I believe I must date it from my first seeing his beautiful grounds at Pemberley.'

Although Elizabeth is joking, there is a degree of truth to what she says. Her life as mistress of Pemberley will ensure her financial stability and allow her to take care of her family. In addition to this she is marrying her equal in intellect, character and affection. Their's will be a marriage based on love, self-knowledge and respect. ✔

Jane Austen's views on an 'ideal' marriage seem to be fulfilled predominantly through the marriages of Jane and Bingley and Elizabeth and Darcy. ✔ The other marriages are lacking in either respect, understanding or love, or in some cases in more than one of these areas. ✔ These two marriages, although clearly neither is perfect, have financial security, partners of 'good character' and, of course, love. ✔ The marriage she leaves us with at the close of the novel is ironically that of the Gardiners. They are not wealthy but he earns a good living as a solicitor, they love one another, have happy, lively children and perhaps most significantly, they have been instrumental in bringing Elizabeth and Darcy together. Their marriage is shown in contrast to the Bennets'. Mr Gardiner as Mrs Bennet's brother is everything she is not and the affection and understanding in their marriage exemplifies this. ✓ Darcy's and Elizabeth's love for them is the final focus of the narrator. They are not satirised or mocked but rather are held up as a further example of a successful marriage. It seems by the end of the novel that there are marriages that Austen approves of and others that are disapproved of, but none that are completely ideal as none of her characters are perfect. ✓

Examiner's comments

This is fundamentally an accomplished piece of writing that examines both potentially successful and unsuccessful marriages. The candidate has a clear understanding of the use of the omniscient narrator but could have focused on Austen's frequent of use of Elizabeth's perspective on events and whether this indicates that Austen's views are shown through Elizabeth more than other characters. Are there areas of Elizabeth's and Darcy's relationship that need working on before their marriage could be seen as ideal?

Quick quiz answers

Quick quiz 1

Who? What? Where? When? Why? How?

1   Elizabeth; she 'has something more of quickness than her sisters' (Ch1)
2   Lydia (Ch9)
3   Lady Catherine de Bourgh (Ch13); she is Darcy's aunt (Ch16)
4   Georgiana Darcy, Darcy's sister (Ch21)
5   He says that she is not handsome enough to tempt him to dance. (Ch3)
6   that her face is rendered intelligent by beautiful eyes, her figure is light and pleasing, her manners are attractively 'playful' (Ch6)
7   (a) His accusations against Darcy are false. (Ch18)
    (b) He makes friends, but may not keep them. (Ch18)
    Both assessments are true.
8   Longbourn; Meryton
9   because their property goes to another relative on Mr Bennet's death; they need financial security (Ch7)
10 clergy must set an example; his happiness; Lady Catherine recommends it (Ch19)
11 relieved; he is more attracted to her than he would like, and Miss Bingley is obviously sensitive to this (Ch12)
12 Elizabeth is disappointed in Charlotte. Mrs Bennet is outraged. Mr Bennet enjoys the foolishness. Jane is charitable. (Ch23)

Who is this?

1   Mr Bennet (Ch1)
2   Mrs Bennet (Ch2)
3   Mr Bingley (Ch3)

Quick quiz 2

Who? What? Where? When? Why? How?

1   Darcy, whose attention seems ambiguous, or Fitzwilliam 'the pleasantest man' (Ch32)
2   his language (her 'inferiority', his 'degradation'); his certainty of being accepted (Ch34)
3   an 'ungentlemanlike' manner; ruining the happiness of Jane and Bingley and exposing both to social derision; reducing Wickham to poverty, ruining his prospects (Ch34)
4   He took £3,000 instead of the living, wasted it, then demanded the living too. (Ch35)
5   She finds in his gentleness 'an affectation and a sameness' and his gallantry 'idle and frivolous'. (Ch41)
6   to London, visiting the Gardiners (Ch25)
7   because he is shy, and not dishonest enough to 'perform to strangers' (Ch31)
8   so that Mr Collins is less tempted to spend a lot of time there (Ch30)
9   to let her expose herself without 'expense or inconvenience to her family'; she will give them no peace, will be in little danger, may learn humility, and couldn't get worse (Ch41)

10 He thought Jane was indifferent. He deplored her lack of connections but also the Bennets' 'total want of propriety'. Darcy feels bad at having concealed Jane's presence in London. (Ch35)

11 respects him, is grateful for his love, sorry for his disappointment, indignant at his manner, does not regret her refusal, or wish to see him again (Ch37)

Who is this?
1 Mr Collins (Ch24)
2 Mrs Gardiner (Ch25)
3 Bingley (Ch24)

Quick quiz 3
Who? What? Where? When? Why? How?
1 Mr Gardiner (Ch49); this is a final underestimation of Darcy, who in fact arranged everything
2 Georgiana Darcy and Bingley (Ch44); this disproves Wickham's reports of her pride, and gives Elizabeth hope for Jane, and even less to hold against Darcy
3 the beauty of the estate, his stature as landowner, his housekeeper's good opinion, his smiling portrait, his civility to the Gardiners (Ch43)
4 Mr Bennet rejects Lydia completely. Mrs Bennet is overjoyed and oblivious to any wrongdoing. (Ch50)
5 renewed hope from Elizabeth's refusal to Lady Catherine, and the warmth of her thanks (Ch58)

6 the assurance that she will never enter into an engagement with Darcy (Ch56)
7 out of doors, walking in the garden (Ch56) or the country (Ch58, 59)
8 He was 'sick of civility, of deference, of officious attention', and admired her 'impertinence'. (Ch60)
9 his debts; he did not intend to marry her, planning a better match abroad (Ch52)
10 She thinks he despises her at the news of Lydia's disgrace; in fact he is moved by her distress. (Ch46)
11 quotes Mrs Reynolds' criticisms; refers to Georgiana's past indiscretion and his unsuitability to 'make sermons'; rejects his complaints about the lost living (Ch52)
12 delighted — talks constantly (Ch55); stuck dumb — then delighted (mainly by Darcy's wealth) (Ch59)

Who is this?
1 Wickham (Ch47)
2 Darcy (Ch43)
3 Lady Catherine (Ch56)

Good luck in your GCSE exams!

Page 14, Jane Austen, © Bettman/Corbis
Page 17, Scene, © Feldman Lauree/Index Stock/Alamy.com

First published 1994
Revised edition 2004

Letts Educational
Chiswick Centre
414 Chiswick High Road
London W4 5TF
Tel: 020 8996 3333

Text © John Mahoney and Stewart Martin 1994
2004 edition revised by Andrea Stowe

Cover and text design by Hardlines Ltd., Charlbury, Oxfordshire.

Typeset by Letterpart Ltd., Reigate, Surrey.

Graphic illustration by Beehive Illustration, Cirencester, Gloucestershire.

Commissioned by Cassandra Birmingham

Editorial project management by Vicky Butt

Printed in Italy.

British Library Cataloguing in Publication Data. A CIP record of this book is available from the British Library.

ISBN 1 84315 324 6

Letts Educational is a division of Granada Learning, part of Granada plc.